The Sparks Opinion

JOEL SPARKS

authorHOUSE®

AuthorHouse™ UK Ltd.
500 Avebury Boulevard
Central Milton Keynes, MK9 2BE
www.authorhouse.co.uk
Phone: 08001974150

©2008 Joel Sparks. All rights reserved.

No part of this book may be reproduced, stored in a retrieval system, or transmitted by any means without the written permission of the author.

First published by AuthorHouse 12/17/2008

ISBN: 978-1-4389-3139-5 (sc)

Printed in the United States of America
Bloomington, Indiana

This book is printed on acid-free paper.

Contents

The Internet: Society's Blood	1
Textisms	3
A Date with Disney	5
10 Lessons from TV & Film	7
The Internet Chat room: Welcome to Hell	9
The Power of the Insult	11
The People History Forgot	13
Monopoly: How It Should Be	15
Before You Clear Your Desk	17
One Track Mind	19
No Ideas Please, We Have Sequels	21
The Kissing Code	23
The Person You Hate	25
Evolution to Destruction	27
Pearls of Wisdom	30
The Office Party	32
A Trip to the Toilet	34
The Power of the Insult II	36
Puberty: The Guantanamo Bay of Life	38
This Is My Status	41
Black Is Better	43
Video Game Your Life	45
The Complaint Consequence	48

The Sober Guy	50
Shows I Watched as a Kid	52
The 13th Day of Christmas	55
RAGE	57
Breakdown of the Break Up	59
I've Got The Power	61
Inside a Blonde's Mind	63
Sleeping With The Accents	65
The High Street Gauntlet	67
Cost of a Crush	69
Immaturity: The Great Cliché	71
Day of the Devil	73
10 Lessons from Cartoons	75
The Ex	77
List of 5	79
Wedding Day Woe	81
Practical Joke Perpetrator	83
The Real Punch Lines	85
Keep It Short	87
The Power of the Insult III	89
The Dating Inquisition	91
Odd One Out	93
Gaseous Maximus	95
We Are Kidding Ourselves	97
If The World Was Going To End	99
10 Lessons from Music	101
49 Things We've Learned	103

The Internet: Society's Blood

AH THE WORLD OF INTERNET social networks... the phenomenon of MySpace has taken over. MySpace was essentially set up as a website where people could share their musical tastes but it has rapidly become one of the biggest websites in the world. Millions of members with their friend's added to their profiles, bands that have gone to huge success on the back of the site and even some MySpace celebrities have been created. It has become a site that everyone has joined and now everyone has cloned...

I have been bombarded by so many invites to such sites that I am now MySpaced Out, Facebooked up, Netlogged In, WAYN'ed, Tagged, Bebo-pped and Linked Up. Oh it's very nice to have a stack of friends and on some sites have them wax lyrical about you. It begs one simple question... why? You might be looking for other people but dropping your profile in the middle of the massive ocean of profiles in a massive website does not make you easier to find.

I reckon it is more out of boredom. You sit there and you are You Tubed to death, you've flicked through File Cabi.net until your fingers bled, Metacafed yourself to sleep and Miniclipped your way through every game. BBC News is telling you nothing new and Google and its mass of options seems as pointless as its search results are abundant. You are ready to MS-eNd it all, say Yahoo to instant messengers and all criminal activities have become boring, as you've Limewired every illegal download in a Bit Torrential storm of piracy.

Welcome to the wonderful world of the internet that is consuming our lives. A world where the most viewed celebrity is the Numa Numa guy, where you can be friends with anyone, as long as they accept you and invites to that website do not automatically go to their Junk Mail Folder. A world where music is free, yet it somehow still funds crime (No one has ever explained how downloading free illegal music aids terrorism. Please send answers on a postcard). It is a place where you can find everything, from the recipe for the perfect meal to the perfect suicide bomb. Where all knowledge is Wiki and all adverts just pop up, rather than waiting for the breaks...

It all started out so simple... now it's the blood coursing through our society's veins...

Textisms

LET ME HIGHLIGHT A GROWING trend in our species that really racks me off! Textisms... confused? Well it's the name I give to things people do in texts that are just plain stupid and annoying. The primary one being the words "he he" being randomly littered through a text. When does anyone ever go "he he" in real life? I could understand if it was something like LOL or ha ha but where the hell did "he he" come from?!

Another one is the desire to fit an X in at the end of every text. You know, unless it was a girlfriend, no other girl kisses me goodbye or at the end of every sentence. Why put the X there then? What is it for? The answer I have had is "It's something I do" or "It's a girl thing." Yeah those are crap answers and display how someone just does stupid things robotically, like stupidity is nature to them.

Other things include put exclamation marks at the end of every sentence. Why do these people need to text like they are saying everything shocked? Texts are not about perfect grammar but talk about no need. Save your thumbs a job and cut the unnecessary exclamation marks. It doesn't make the text seem more interesting or lively.

Also the text conversation is something that bewilders me. If you want to have a conversation, try calling me. But some people think that's less fun. I don't see how really. I would much rather talk to someone face to face. If not that, I like to hear their voice. Texts for me are for quick basic info, to save the hassle of a long call (ask my friends; I am the master of the one word text message). When texting starts becoming a conversation that defeats the object. It also sucks up all my free texts and I have to reply or the sender thinks I hate their guts.

Either way, they are stupid little conventions we have all picked up. I find myself doing them and wonder "why why why?!" Textisms show just what a bored, stupid bunch we are. We need to find something better to do! QUICK!

A Date with Disney

THE THINGS YOU TALK ABOUT when you are bored. Recently I had a discussion with a number of friends on which Disney girl you would date. Now ignoring the fact that these are two dimensional beings that are purely the work of some geek, stuck behind an easel or computer, there are many options available. Surprisingly it can prove to be a fairly divisive argument. However, I have the correct answer and let me explain why...

Clearly Belle from Beauty and the Beast is the only option. Yes she is French... Yes she is a nerd that does nothing but reads... Yes she goes for a hairy beast over the big hunk. You might think those are drawbacks but no. She might be French but after checking that she does shave her pits and washes on a regular basis, then we can get past that. She does have an American accent after all. Yes she reads a lot but a bimbo is not an option anyways. She chooses the hairy beast over the hunk means even someone as simple as me has a chance. As you can see, she is the right choice.

Ariel (The Little Mermaid) is just not an option. Whilst the whole sea shell attire would inspire lust in any man, the fish tail is going to be a problem. And even if she manages to get legs in a remarkable trade up from the fish tail, let's be honest... she is a ginger. Fit or not, it would lead to ginger children that would be mocked on school playgrounds for years. You have got to think long term sometimes.

Jasmine, Aladdin's main squeeze, is the rich little madam. Now sure she wants the street rat and that might seem very honourable. But you do realise what that means? She likes to go for the bad guy. You know the type, the scum bag loser that will play her for a fool but she'll want him for the thrill, saying "I can change him." This type is best avoided!

Esmeralda from The Hunchback of Notre Dame is dirty. You just couldn't be seen in public with her.

Mulan... come on... I don't care what anyone tells me. She is a dyke and probably a lesbian.

Snow White and Cinderella... they are a bit old.

Nala (from The Lion King) was said based on her sexy voice (!) The individual who said it looked very ashamed after saying it. Now we know what he does with his weekends!!

Megara in Hercules... she was a close call but she sold her man down the river to Hades. Proof that women are men's downfall and therefore ruling her out. Belle brought about the Beast's salvation where as Megara just made life more difficult for Hercules. He was only trying to become a god after all!

Pocahontas is in essence a decent option. However, do you really want to have to go out, hunt down and kill 4 buffalo, haul them in front of her father just as payment for the first date? This is the type that would burn a hole in your pocket (if she had any concept of currency and economics). She doesn't use cash or credit cards and already she is proving to be high maintenance. Just wait until she discovers High Street shopping and your life and bank balance will plummet.

I think you can see my point. If Jessica Rabbit had been a Disney creation, she would have been a serious contender but the fact is that if you are going to have a date with Disney, it might as well be with Belle.

10 Lessons from TV & Film

Here are 10 lessons we should take from the world of TV and film:-

1. If you are going to make a TV show about a load of people stranded on a desert island, don't just make it up as you go along. After one or two seasons, people will come to realise that it sucks and there is no real plot. People love mystery but a few decent answers now and then never hurt.

2. Don't be friends with Jessica Fletcher (the lady from Murder, She Wrote). The reality is that you will end up either dead or under suspicion of killing someone. The upside of being the prime suspect is that inevitably she will find the real killer to get you off the hook. No wonder there is so much crime. The only people who can solve murders in the US are Jessica Fletcher, Reverend Dowling, Quincy and Dick Van Dyke. An author, a vicar, a forensic scientist and a doctor!

3. If you know a man called Jack Bauer, you will be kidnapped and tortured at some point in your life. As traumatic as it is, you will be expected to pull yourself together and be back working within the hour. There is no time to be pulling a sickie when you've had a drill inserted in your shoulder! Get back to work or you won't make the next season!

4. The Government and other shadowy organisations have plenty of people who are hired to absorb bullets for more important people.

Unless your name is close to the title of the show or film, you can't shoot straight and you are always the fool who forgot to wear a bulletproof vest.

5. When you don't have enough interesting things going on in your life, a montage piece to a quality piece of music smoothes over that gap.

6. Bombs cannot be diffused until ten seconds before detonation.

7. No wedding can happen without some tragedy coming to the forefront. Whether it be the previous husband showing up alive or the wedding being bombed, something always comes up. It suddenly makes the dilemmas of "are flowers in place?" and "is the Best Man sober?" pale in comparison.

8. The UN can send an entire army to solve a problem and it will take years. Send one man with one weapon against a legion of terrorists and with some quick thinking and a handy sidekick, he will obliterate all of them. And all villains in the world are Arabian or English. It is just the English do a better job of masquerading as other nationalities.

9. Every hospital has a fiercely cynical doctor, who is an unbearable human being most of the time but his encyclopedic medical knowledge makes him indispensable. Hope that he is yours because whilst his bed side manner will make you feel as small as an ant, chances are he has never lost a patient.

10. No matter how gripping and action packed an episode is, it can still be pretty much covered in 2 minutes, as long as someone with an imposing voice says "Previously on…" just before the clip shown before next week's show.

The Internet Chat room: Welcome to Hell

IN A TIME WHEN HALLE Berry, one of the most beautiful women in the world, admitted that she regularly goes on chat rooms to gain anonymity and a private life with it, those that have frequented such places regularly will know that they are addictive yet hellish places. You know already the brand of people that are in there and if you honestly thought about it, you would come to the realisation that it is effectively a trip to Hades' electronic habitat. Even Halle Berry has bemoaned how it didn't really provide the solace she desired but in fact, she found rejection and mockery when she revealed her true self.

What kind of people go regularly into chat rooms? Well the primary group that we instantly associate with chat rooms is the deviants, ones of the sexual varieties. You know the type I mean, paedophiles looking for 14 year olds to groom, guys looking to get on cam and show their... stuff (Dirty Den style)... and of course the guys pretending to be girls. There is getting in touch with your feminine side but what they are actually after is, well, better provided by Mills & Boon. So why on earth would you go in one? There are cybernetic child molesters, deviants and trannies that only do it under disguise of a lewd username.

OK that is possibly a little extreme. What other kind of people lurk in there apart from shy Hollywood stars? Bots! Programs purely designed to advertise various sites, most unpleasant and rife with viruses and no doubt, porn. Somehow this is not redeeming the seedy situation the chat room finds itself in. It does seem to be the sanctuary of the socially inept and sexually desperate!

But then there are the other people. The cheeky people, who go into chat rooms to see if anyone can email them music for free. Surely this must be a dying breed! The world of Peer to Peer file sharing and cheap mp3 download websites means that associating with this crowd is no longer necessary but if you go into a chat room and you will still find them.

Along with them, is people looking to pick a fight. Now I have been into a UK chat room where a French person had foolishly wandered in to proclaim France as the greatest country in the world. He was swiftly joined by an American, who was as patriotic as he was stupid. Suddenly within minutes, I was awash in a sea of rage, racism, xeno and homophobia. It wasn't pleasant, as they turned on everyone who admitted to being black, Muslim, gay or female. Had I known that I had infiltrated a chat room of the KKK (or the BNP as they are now known) I would have not bothered sticking around or even going in.

Finally it is the people that are the ones to avoid at all the costs! The lonely depressives! The kind who are there to wallow and are not interested in making the world better. They have found their forum for moaning and nothing will stop them. We used to be able to channel such people into phone lines but now they have a worldwide audience. Now the platform of the chat room is free to promote porn, promiscuity, pity, pro-Nazi views and piracy.

So why does a gorgeous film star feel the urge to go in a chat room? Halle Berry said she went in to find a life and no wonder she was disappointed. It is full of all these hideous characters in there. If you want this in your life, I suggest leaving the chat room and moving to a chav estate. At least, when the conversation runs dry, you can go burn a car or smash a bus shelter.

The Power of the Insult

THERE IS NOTHING QUITE AS satisfying as a well timed, eloquently worded, vicious insult. I know you have that nice person inside you saying "What a terrible thing to say!" but admit it, when it comes off it is very empowering. You feel smart, the person who needed to be put in their place has been, what's not to like? Sure people will talk bad about you but it's better to be hatefully remembered than totally forgotten. Thinking back, I thought it would be best to note down my best insults, so generations of time will not think they are being original but merely plagiarising me. I'd love someone to start a line "I believe Sparks put it best when he said…" Nothing says you've made the big time like someone adding the copyright owner of the phrase to the insult to make it that little more condescending… so please enjoy and quote at your leisure

- You've got the look of a George model

- Not even squatters would move into that empty skull of yours

- A evening with a shotgun and suicidal tendencies would be more fun than going out with you

- People don't think you're stupid. The fact you're ugly distracts them from that

- I'd say you were going to Hell but I am starting to think you're the one leasing it to Satan

- If you got hit by a bus tomorrow, I'd be upset... because I wasn't driving!

- When your IQ hits double figures, sell it!

- You have the directional sense of a Marine in Iran

- How deep under the scalp does your "blonde" go?

- You know when you were born; did your Mum keep the receipt?

- You don't have to be alone. I know plenty of people who think highly of you and would be willing to give you all the time, love and understanding you would ever want. They are called therapists.

- You can't miss him... he is the one causing the eclipse

- He's as straight as a roundabout!

- I'm offended by the fact that you are alive... it means you are stealing my oxygen!

- His career potential can be summed up by the phrase "Do you want fries with that?"

The People History Forgot

History... dictated by those who won, those who are still standing and those who could put across the most convincing story. How most of history has any credibility is beyond me. It is full of bias and we take it as true based on some of the details proving to be true. As long as the history teller can link the truth logically, he can hammock those facts with as many lies as he or she wants. However, the one fact of history I would love to know is about those forgotten people in history. The people who did not realise that history and with it a Hollywood re-telling, celluloid style with vast inaccuracies, beckoned to immortalise them with box office sales and an Oscar to boot.

People like...

The innkeeper that turned Mary and Joseph away in the story of the Nativity. Can you imagine the business he could have got with the claim that divinity had been born in his place? That beats any star rating the AA can dish out!

The guy who put an arrow in King Harold's eye. No doubt he reeled away to a loving, wild crowd like an English football striker slamming home a 35 yard shot into the top corner of the net.

The architect of the pyramids. He drew up plans and helped orchestrate the establishment of one of the Wonders of the World and he didn't even get a tiny little sign on one of them. They didn't even name one after him. Now, in this celebrity-infested name-dropping society we live in, I'm pretty sure when a post box or a park bench is erected, it gets a nice gold plated sign put on it, dedicating it to someone. And you know his only payment was to avoid being whipped for another day.

The guy who left his oven on and started the Great Fire of London. Now he must have felt awful. He had taken one of the great cities of the world and burned a huge chunk of it down. Now history would have, at first, painted him a fool and then a saviour. He helped the city get rid of a large amount of dross and build better things to replace the old. We need people like this man in every chav town, from Hull to Southend. It would be much more effective than ASBOs.

And finally... the guy who invented reality TV. Had he known what kind of tripe he would subsequently bring onto our screens, he might have thought again. With that said, maybe that is why his name is not in history. Either he made himself totally disappear or the Government found him and eradicated all trace of him.

History has far too many forgotten people to be taken seriously!

Monopoly: How It Should Be

Monopoly conducted a vote on their website as they aim to make a UK Edition of Monopoly, with the top towns making it onto the board. I know that every town has pretty much got its own edition but I do think that the game makers have missed a chance to make the games a bit more authentic. I offer these only as suggestions and of course, there will be some who disagree (probably people who live in the towns I mention) but this is purely my insight.

The Liverpool edition would be predominantly filled with "Go to Jail" squares and the car piece would have the wheels missing. Instead of passing Go, it would be passing the Social Security office.

Brighton edition would be one where all the streets are pink and everyone would get £200 for passing "Oh Stop"

Hull would have an edition, however, it is all boarded up and mortgaged off.

Manchester has all the traditional elements but you are required to get past Moss Side or you may receive the mandatory stab wound. Also the pieces would be replaced with a gun, a knife, a syringe and a teenage gangster.

Glasgow would be put into an authentic version of Monopoly but it is impossible to create a board game that even the residents can get lost driving around, so it would have to be shelved anyway.

Or you could have the Leeds edition, except it wouldn't be about gathering enough properties but enough terrorist cells to start a Jihad. The houses and hotels would merely be used to symbolise how much property damage you intended to do.

Finally you could create a North Wales edition. You would just buy streets to see how many speed cameras you would set up. However, you could only charge rent (or a fine) if the person screamed past your monopoly. Pieces would include a buffoon Chief Constable, a symbol of a STI and a fluffy sheep.

OK these are all a bit harsh... but Monopoly would be seriously funny if they just randomly turned one of these out!

Before You Clear Your Desk

RECENTLY I HAVE SERIOUSLY CONTEMPLATED quitting my job. It's not the worst job in the world and the pay is ok. However, it can be fairly mundane, the career prospects are a little poor and I have a departmental boss that makes Medusa look like a friendly little schoolgirl. It was out of a desire to actually go and do something I have always wanted to do but like most of the rest of the world, being part of such a system means having the safety net of money coming into the bank. Needless to say I am still in my job and won't quit until something better becomes available. It did, however, get me thinking about what you could do in those last few days at work before you clear your desk.

The controversy that you could court! It's better to be controversial than forgotten. For example, you could call up the IT helpdesk and tell them you can't seem to get on to any porn sites. Insist that it is purely work related.

Spread a rumour around work that you saw the fat girl scanning her naked backside on the photocopier. Watch as people approach the photocopier, only to change their mind and walk away, repulsed by the idea of being contaminated by butt crack perspiration.

Change your name badge by putting a Post It note over it with the message "You and me are not on first name terms... GOT IT?!" (You ever notice how if you call staff in a shop by their first name, they pull a face that says "How did you know my name?" Duh! You're wearing it!)

eave a note on the disabled parking space that asks "Why does this guy have a wheel coming out of his bum?"

Leave a note by the No Smoking sign that reads "Yeah, keep your cancer to yourself!"

Call up the secretary of the MD or CEO and ask "How do you feel about him cheating on you with his wife?"

Go to work with your underwear over your clothes, insisting it is part of religious beliefs. Look very upset if anyone laughs at the idea of the Church of Superman and lodge complaint with Human Resources about religious discrimination.

Call up the complaints department and tell them that they are a bunch of moaners. Ask why they never have anything nice to say about anything. Tell them that their job description is a lousy excuse and they should turn their frowns upside down.

Send an email to all users asking if anyone has seen your pen. Be vague, await the lack of response and then email all users again, telling them they are all heartless. Remind them that the one pen is just as important as the 99 pens left in the box. Sign the email off with the letters WWJD

Call the company's pension scheme and inform them that you suffer from a condition that means you age in dog years and so technically you have been over 65 for some time. Ask for the missed payments in a lump sum.

Tell your boss what you really think of them. Tell the person you fancy in work that not only do you think they are hot but their hotness has been magnified 10 times because they brighten up what is usually a rubbish day. All these things would definitely mean you would go out with a bang! Before you clear your desk, leave a big muddy footprint in the company you used to work for, if you want to get rid of the safety net. Chances are you will walk the tightrope of opportunity more determined if you do. When you do that, then you are really living the dream and all power to those who do.

One Track Mind

Apparently men think about one thing and one thing only. That is what the all knowing half of the human species, namely the ladies, say. I hear that a friend of mine put an advert in the local paper, selling his 26 volumes of encyclopedias for £1000. He was looking for a quick sale as they were no longer needed. He had got married and it turns out that his wife knows everything. But seriously, the amount of times I have heard a woman utter the words "Men... one track mind" shows how little women know us. I don't say this to deride women. In fact, I openly proclaim they are superior to men. They are generally more intelligent, more beautiful and more ambitious than us men. This is not to flatter, that is just the facts, not including the vast amount of "blonde moments" they all have and their inability to deal with directions or read maps.

The one track they speak of... we're all adults here. Sex. The one track of a male mind is sex (or action of some form... sometimes a random snog is enough) according to the intellectually superior women. Ladies, you let yourselves down with such a line. Not only does it prove that you are not mind readers, which half the time you expect us to be, but it shows how you know nothing about men and so therefore you can not criticise us.

Trust me, that is not the first thing on our minds. Stick a load of guys in a room and 99% of the time, that topic will not get the ball rolling. Sports will and if it is any sport, football is going to top the bill most of the time. From there it will be cars, films, probably beer, stupid jokes we have heard and then possibly good looking girls. Chances are by then, most men are drunk and the conversation has become as incoherent as a Party Political broadcast.

OK so it's not a vast amount of topics that are generally covered but it illustrates the point. Men do not focus their lives on sex. In fact, my Granddad taught me, wise man that he was, that a plate of steak and chips will satisfy you just as much. Now I don't know how much comfort to take from that but it does make me wonder if I should have a bottle of ketchup ready on my wedding night, just in case seasoning is needed. However, he makes a valid point. Men take pleasure in the simple things of life.

I know men who say watching their football team win a certain trophy was the greatest moment of their lives. These are happily married men with children and successful careers and they say watching some guy lift a big cup is the best moment. Or a guy that said bungee jumping is better than sex. To be fair, when he told me that, my first thought was "Because the bungee jump lasted longer?" And of course, the trip to Alton Towers and going on one of its vast array of roller coasters was better than "doing it." Well lining up for an hour for a rollercoaster of 45 seconds of thrill seeking fun, at least the waiting time is significantly better. OK yes, at times, we are pigs and deserve the cheek we get.

However, among all this, let's say we did have this one track mind. It puts women at the front of our minds. You become the core of our desires and is that really that bad? As long as we are respectful and control our urges, we are just desiring to be with a superior, beautiful human being. The problem being you think we want you just for your body... it's not true. Only drunken fools do that! The rest of us are smart enough to know that we will have to talk to you in the morning. But more importantly, not only must you be a person we enjoy being around but you need to be able to cook a good plate of steak and chips! We've got to have some kind of satisfaction in this!

Just kidding ladies... I love you all. Not enough respect is given to womanhood these days and too often people try to devalue and degrade what is the supreme creation on this rock. Just don't be too hard on us. We are doing our best!

No Ideas Please, We Have Sequels

NOTHING SAYS YOU'VE RUN OUT of ideas, fear creativity and are just in it for the money quite like churning out a sequel. Every year we get to summer and we complain about how it is a year of sequels, like it hasn't happened a million times before. Whilst it might seem that I am not a fan of sequels, that is not the case. I think if a character is interesting enough and the story is worth telling, then make a sequel, make a trilogy, make a franchise out of it. I have enjoyed watching James Bond over the decades in numerous films. I don't want them to stop and I don't think they should stop making good sequels. Just don't make sequels for the sake of it.

Sequels tend to be inferior on the basis that the surprise element is taken out of it. When The Matrix came out, it blew everyone away. We had never seen anything like it. Then it's sequels came out and it was trashed and generally thrown out as a money making exercise. Maybe it was but I still wish my money making exercises were even half as profitable! However, once the idea was suggested that The Matrix could have a sequel, the studio was not going to miss an opportunity and the public went wild for the idea. It would have seemed more stupid to reject the suggestion, so they got made. It makes me wonder which sequels never quite made it...

Gladiator 2: The Revenge - Maximus is reincarnated as a mighty warrior, hell bent on gaining further revenge. Strangely though, instead of a trusty sword and shield, he is handed a massive cotton bud to fight his battles. With Ulrika Jonsson guiding him through it and probably sleeping with him too, he will have to face his ultimate fate... the dreaded travellator!

Independence Day: The Day After Tomorrow - Will Smith et al start the clear up operation of having all these alien craft burning on the planet. However, they don't realise that the carbon emissions from the flaming ships has accelerated global warming so quickly, that we get hit by every freak storm and the world freezes over in a new ice age. A new set of aliens invade on ice skates and Al Gore releases the sequel to "An Inconvenient Truth" called "Don't Want to Say I Told You So But"

School of Rock 2: The Remake - Jack Black suddenly realises that most of his comedy movies are rehashes of his old ones and so returns to one of his most successful films and does the same jokes but this time with more explosions and a higher body count. After seeing the success of this film, The Waterboy 2, Anchorman 2 and Dodgeball 2 are all commissioned.

Lethal Weapon 5 - Mel Gibson and Danny Glover are reunited yet again, with half the script being about how they are not too old. They say that but all action sequences have to be halted halfway through, so the pair of them can take a toilet break.

With a mind like mine, I should be a studio executive! I could churn out celluloid rubbish, hyping it like it was the greatest epic of all time, make my money and then move on to the next one. Hey Rupert Murdoch! Hire me!

The Kissing Code

THE WORLD IS RAPIDLY BECOMING homogenised. Things are becoming regulated, censored and codified, dictating to us how things should be and how things should go. Whilst I don't like to be told that I can't hold or express certain opinions, that I have to stress because of the excess salt, fat or E numbers in my food or that indeed my social life will not be complete without a rough knowledge of mediocre soap operas and tortuous reality TV shows, there is room for rules in this world.

So it has come to that time, when we as a people need to establish rules about the more important things in life... that's right. Kissing. Smooching, snogging, tonsil tennis, tongue tussling, checking for fillings, you can call it what you want. We've all had that excitement leading up to the kiss and then the experience of the kiss itself. No doubt we have also had bitter disappointments with some instances. So now we need some rules for it!

First of all, offering the cheek. Ladies, if a guy has got that close and then to get out of it, you offer your cheek rather than your lips, you've lead him on. No guy, barring a drunk, just dives in. It can make you feel like total rubbish too. So gentlemen, I propose that cheek offerers are blacklisted, with the punishment of chapped lips and cold sores with no cream to soothe their pain. If they are not going to use them pouters, they might as well carry the lip afflictions of the world.

Secondly, kissing is not a lip sport. It is far deeper than that. Keeping your mouth closed during a kiss makes it feel gross. It makes it feel like you're kissing your Mum good night. I know you are already shuddering at the thought! Closed mouth kisses can only be exchanged by blood family members. In the southern United States, closed mouth kissing is totally outlawed... but I don't think we'll follow that example. Like they say, you might be a redneck if it takes you 5 minutes to kiss your cousin goodbye.

Third on my list, slobbering is a criminal offence. Having been on the wrong end of a slobber smoocher, I am pretty sure it constitutes attempted murder, as she tried to drown me in saliva. Sure a little bit is needed to keep the machinery going. I've been in instances where the make out session has been going on so long, where I had to stop, get a quick drink to replenish the stocks, so we could both get back to it. So slobbering is not only criminal, it's wasteful. Just think how long we could have gone on if you weren't drooling like a rabid dog!

Fourth, biting is good when soft. Biting that draws blood is exclusively the domain of vampires. Hickeys are the grey area. They are made out to be disgusting but you know what, I don't see why. Last time I had a hickey, my mates at work tried to wind me up. My reaction was "Yes a beautiful woman sucked on my neck... jealous?!" Therefore, only beautiful women can give hickeys. Ugly women hickeys will always be described as "cut myself shaving."

Fifth, teeth clashing is not the end of the world but repeated cases are just rude. It is no mystery where a person's teeth are. Why are you trying to get that deep anyway? It's a kiss, not the tongue equivalent of the javelin! This is not a trip to the dentists. You hit the teeth, back it up a little!

And finally, giggling through a kiss because you are nervous means the ultimate punishment. You will be made to go through puberty again, spots, zits, stupid haircuts and school uniforms, the lot. If you are going to act like a 14 year old, you need to be treated like one. However, it does also mean the guy you were kissing will have to be considered for the paedophile list, since he was making out with a child!

Kissing can be fun. It can be a casual thing or a deep meaningful thing. Just don't make it a painful or awkward!

The Person You Hate

I AM THE PERSON YOU hate.

I am the employee of the month when you are getting a verbal warning for shopping on the internet during work hours.

I am the one who shows up in the same outfit as you to every party you ever attend. And I always look better than you.

I'm the person who says the punch line of the joke you're telling before you get to the end.

I'm the one who saw the big movie of the summer before you. And I will probably tell you the twist ending before you get chance to see it for yourself

I'm the driver who cuts you up in traffic and then looks at you like you need to be in an institution, as you vent your inevitable road rage with words and possibly the crowbar in the boot of your car.

I'm the guy who breaks girl's hearts but still gets them all, when you can't find action in a randy nightclub riddled with rohypnol.

I'm the studio executive that cuts your favourite show on TV because only 300,000 other people want to watch with you.

I'm the radio DJ that keeps talking over your favourite song.

I'm French.

I'm the muscle bound Adonis in the gym when you walk in with more spare tyres than Michelin.

I'm the guy who wins at everything, even though you are better than me at everything and anything. Don't worry, second place just says that of all the losers, you were the best.

I'm the guy who is better than you and you think I'm so arrogant. Not that it is instantly obnoxious and arrogant for you to assume that no one can be better than you.

I'm the guy driving by in my Ferrari when your Vauxhall is shaking to pieces.

Whoever you hate, don't waste your time. They don't bother wasting their time with you!

Evolution to Destruction

HUMANS. WE'RE SO EVOLVED. So superior. Yes we are the pinnacle of the evolutionary stage, being the most intelligent of nature's creations. People can say monkeys and dolphins are intelligent creatures but frankly none of them invented the DVD player or toasted sandwich maker! Yes we are a race, a species better than the rest...

Yeah right! Who are we trying to kid? Can you see the sheer stupidity of the world? We build our society and claim that we want to have a fair spread of wealth, that poverty has no place in this day and age. We then wait for over paid self publicising celebrities to lead us into the fight. That is modern day equivalent of getting Martin Luther King to get Hitler to fight for his cause! Inaction and apathy are so much easier standards to live by. Maybe you were one of the fools who put your name down as part of the Live 8 protest. Of course you did it to benefit Africa and who came out best for it all? Pink Floyd and The Who! Their album sales rocket, money is still thrown ineffectively at Africa and we feel better about ourselves. Sure the kids are dying and all but it gives us an excuse for another good charity concert in the near future.

Talking of reasons to have a charity gig, we stress about how we are warming up the planet and how it is all going to hell. I don't see the problem with global warming myself. So the waters rise 20ft... that means the beach will be closer to my home and the chav coastal towns will be obliterated. Warmer climates, so it does mean less snow but I'll live. Apparently cows farting is causing major problems in the atmosphere too. You know I don't see any of them trying to hold them in because they worry about climate based disasters. They love to flatulate their way through the day. Suggest that Al Gore! Everybody stop farting for a day, save the ozone!

You have to love the stupidity of those two issues contradicting though. We are willing to spend millions on saving the ozone. We'll spend a ton of money on looking at stars 3 million light years away from us. What are we doing with that? Hoping that we can see ET waving back since he phoned home? We spend millions on digging up skeletons of lizards that existed millions of years ago and for what? That kid in Africa is still dying. Dinosaurs and space should be saved for Hollywood and kids toys. I bet with a bit of imagination, they would find a way to combine them!

We're so evolved that we live in a society that wants to share the wealth but then not protect the weak. We tell people that they can do what they want and as long as they don't hurt anyone else, their actions are fine. Sure, a girl can go get plastered and have sex, get pregnant and just abort the pregnancy because she is not ready to be a mother. Because the foetus doesn't vote on Big Brother, contribute taxes and know how to text, that innocent life that did nothing wrong is now expendable. The validation is, of course, that the mother can not provide suitable care for that child. Ah if we used the justification that if we can not care for something adequately we should just kill it, then bring me a shotgun and a chest of shotgun shells. We have a stack of homeless and old people to take out.

I understand that there are instances were such an act like abortion should take place and I think men are just as stupid thinking they can avoid responsibility because if they can't be caught up with, the responsibility doesn't exist. The casual and foolish attitude is what it is all about. We think we are evolving by getting better at something. Like taking Concorde, the fastest passenger plane in the world, and trading it in for a Super Jumbo Jet, so we can shop whilst we travel. Why bother with invention and innovation when you can have retail therapy? We are not getting better; we are getting lazy and stuck in the rut of decadence and depravity. As long as we have our great concerts, quality shopping and no worry that any commitment can be palmed off or erased with a quick procedure that requires two signatures and proof of identity, we are a happy bunch of devolving fools.

Anyone without cash is expendable. Anyone without a vote is expendable. Anyone who doesn't fit the specifications of acceptability in society, whether they be ugly, challenged or born in the wrong place at the wrong time is expendable. The most evolved of the species? We barely win it by opposable thumbs! We are not evolved. We are not even awake. We are the perfect example of evolution to destruction.

Pearls of Wisdom

Wisdom is a word used for that piece of information that goes in one ear, passes swiftly by any active grey matter and then fires out of the other ear. People have tried to overcome this by recording them instead, in the hope that someone will pick it up, read it and learn from it. Stuff like the Bible, the Koran, The World According to Clarkson; these are the texts that keep these pearls of wisdom. So here are mine...

Blonde is not a hair colour, it's a lifestyle

Nothing is left to chance, everything is left to choice

Never go back for seconds (unless its unlimited buffet and the pizzas don't have sweet corn or pineapple on them. Toppings of the devil I tell you)

Fear is pride in pretty clothing

Whatever it takes, do what must be done

A bad yesterday is no excuse for making today worse

Never judge a film by its book

Losing is not an option

Take a compliment and never rebuke a kind intent

First impressions are usually wrong

A day spent texting means you need to get out more

Your head knows, your heart understands

There is no promotion on the dole

Scientists don't know everything but at least they are working on it

Philosophy is not about answering questions, it is about finding a more interesting question to contemplate

Even atheists blame God for all the bad things that happen

Stereotypes have a spine of truth and flesh of falsehood

Even apathy requires dedication

Don't marry someone just for their personality. You are going to have to wake up to that face many times

Love is the reason for living

Passion is positive slavery

Entertaining lies are always more believable than honest truths

Winners never say "It's the taking part that counts"

Sometimes you have to pick the lesser of two evils. It's called a General Election

Stupid people don't understand. Clever people don't understand and then ask for clarification

These are my pearls of wisdom. Use them wisely, as wisdom can result in glorification or devastation, depending upon its application.

The Office Party

There comes a time when we all have to attend one. That's right, the office party. The one where you and your work mates get together under one roof, most of them get heavily inebriated and then make absolute fools of themselves. As for me, I'm the guy who is teetotal and there to enjoy himself, ready with a camera for that opportune "blackmail material" photo. They are the domain of shame, where people get too drunk and end up in a fight or kissing someone that they later regret. So here are a few tips from the guy who didn't have a drop to drink at the office party...

Take your own camera. It sounds like a common sense thing to say but there is a good reason for it. When someone else has a camera, they take a picture of you sat next to the person who happens to be there at the time and that might not be someone you want to be seen with on the latest photo album on some social network website. When you take your camera, you go up to some of the most gorgeous women (or handsome men if you're a girl) in the office and ask to have your picture with them. You will look like a love machine and will be the envy of the office come Monday morning.

Be the first to get the helium balloons. Every office party has them. Be the first to get them and use them for the chipmunk squeaky voice gag. Once someone has done it, you will find it becomes less funny quite quickly. It is usually because there is only so much you can say whilst sounding like a hyperactive Bee Gee that actually is funny.

Do not sit next to the most confident woman in the office. She is usually in her late 30's or early 40's and she will probably ask the waiter to leave the bottle of wine, promptly neck that bottle's contents like it's oxygen and then feel the inclination to flash her boobs. Saggy sacks of flesh are not a view I want for a Friday night and I'm sure you are the same. Unless Wayne Rooney is reading this.

When going to the toilet, use a cubicle. At least then you can lock the door behind you. You won't have to watch someone come in and be sick or separate a fight with your bits and pieces hanging out. It is amazing how the men's toilet goes from a restroom to a Fight Club arena. Yet over in the girl's toilet, it has turned into the latest version of a Roman Forum, carefully debating the vital issues of who to make a move on and make up touch ups, armed with Revlon mascara.

Don't argue with someone who asks you to join them on the dance floor. Join them for at least one song, even if you don't want to. If you don't, it will become a careful campaign to recruit you to the dance floor by all the drunken women on the dance floor. Chances are you will be dragged up just in time for the Time Warp, Macarena or even worse the YMCA. I don't know why people would say no. Everyone is drunk and you can be sure that someone else is dancing worse than you ever could. Chances are 2 minutes later that same person will be flat on their backside too.

And finally, the kiss. A lucky person will get the snog to wrap up the night. Choose wisely for goodness sake because whilst you are busily enjoying it, a dozen people are already formulating the wind ups, the teasing and the gossip that comes attached with it. Pick someone you can be smug about and someone who doesn't sit next to you. The awkward silence that comes from the Monday morning aftermath of that kiss is excruciating.

However, whatever you do, don't miss it! It will fuel the office with conversation for weeks and you do not want to be out of the circle. So go, enjoy and party like Monday morning will never come.

A Trip to the Toilet

LET ME TELL YOU ABOUT an awkward situation I got into once. There I am, bladder absolutely bursting and at the point where conscious thought is slipping away. I walk into this restaurant and storm into the toilets. I didn't notice how nice they were or the fact that there were no urinals. I just took a stall, locked myself in and promptly unloaded a waterfall and probably half of my intestines into the toilet. Finally, I started to get my senses together and I realised that the reason there were no urinals is because women can't stand up when they pee. That's right, I had strolled into the Ladies toilets! I knew this because two ladies were chatting away outside my cubicle. I sat there quietly, listening and waiting for them to leave; I got a quick insight to what happens in the Ladies toilets. It's not a rest room, it's a war room! Where women discuss the events of the evening and the tactics and plans for the rest of the night. It made me think about what happens in the bath room, where your body gets its relief and your mind wanders off into the wilderness. It makes you forget all the possible questions a trip to the toilet should possibly raise.

Now here is a question for you. How do you wipe? This might sound ridiculous but when you have dropped your guts in the pan, how do you clean up? There are a few options. There is the classic side wipe, where you lean over and arch a bit and wipe. Then there is the back hand scoop, shifting forward on the seat a bit, so you can sneak the paper direct to the spot. There is the stand and wipe for those who don't want the toilet seat getting in the way. Now I had one friend insist the front wipe is the only option. His exact line was "it gets it in just the right spot" which made me go "EW!" as I am sure it has made you do the same. How on earth can a front wipe method work? Even if you can reach, the dangers that come with the follow through of the wipe could be gross, as well as unhygienic.

Then there is, for us men, a dilemma at the urinal. You see, women seem think to think that peeing standing up is an exact science. They think that when we write our names in the snow (and come on, which of us hasn't?) it is such an easy task that it should be a calligrapher's masterpiece. Let me tell you ladies, it is not that simple. And then there is the finish. Just like wiping, we have a few options open to us. There is the Maraca technique, where you just shake it like a Polaroid picture. The toothpaste method, where you start at the bottom and gently squeeze upwards. Some just go to a cubicle, get some paper and dab away. Others do the Dad Dance Move of just jiggling on the spot.

Already you can see that the toilets offer a multitude of possibilities and grotesqueries. If it's your own bathroom, maybe you have a mirror, which also substitutes for puss collector for the time when you have a zit that just needs to be popped. The best kind is the ones you get high on your back that have got so big they are starting to hurt. You get a good look at it in the mirror before getting your nails ready at pincer position and squeeze. Sure enough, it bursts and the puss shoots out! And it feels so good! It's up there with relieving yourself when you had been bursting to pee.

It's an odd place the bath room. You can have some of your most profound and creative thoughts sat on the toilet. That is because you have never considered these issues. Your body just goes into auto pilot and your mind is looking for something to do. Just don't let your mind disappear in this equation; you don't want to be walking into the wrong toilet!

The Power of the Insult II

I know this will come as a shock to you but I am fiercely opinionated. If the meek really will inherit the Earth, then I am not even holding out on the hope of taking ownership of a pebble from this planet. Why is that? Because in my life, I come across some people that annoy me so much and the only way I can deal with them even breathing is to put them in their place. Hence the good quality insults. I have seen Jimmy Carr live and he is the king of insults. He just rips out the stupidity of a soul and then slaps the host of it across the face with the raw truth of it. It is genius! That person realises they truly serve no greater purpose than to put carbon dioxide in the air, so the trees feel more useful. No one has told them that cars and power stations do the job better than them, just in case it prompts mass suicide. So, like all good things these days, here is the sequel to the list of great insults The Sparks has mustered over the years.

- Go back to that ugly tree you fell out of and fix all the branches you broke on the way down

- I don't think she has a virus or infection. Even diseases have better taste than that

- The only reward you should get for your work is a P45

- Are you the product of radiation testing?

- Who let this freak escape the circus?

- Tell me, is your profile picture on Facebook a police mug shot? And if so, when is it getting added to the sex offenders' website?

- They'll put a wounded horse down to end its misery, so why won't they put you down to end my misery?

- How I wish your mother had been barren her whole life

- You should look forward to your funeral. On that day, you'll be popular

- You know when I first met you, I had many misconceptions about you. How I treasure them now.

- Who lit the fuse on your tampon?!

- Why is no one attracted to you? The laws of physics dictate that gravity is attracted to you but even that is considering an appeal to the judge

- When I see him I think "Why haven't they pushed that poor beached whale back out to sea?"

- I'd rather be trapped in a room with a cannibal, covered in barbeque sauce, than spend the evening with you

- You validate my inherent mistrust in the human race

Puberty: The Guantanamo Bay of Life

I regularly hear people exclaiming "I wish I was a kid again" and I understand why. They want to go back to the simple life of toys, 9am to 3pm days and no real serious dilemmas. However, I do think these people have not really thought this idea out because if they became kids again, they would have to go through the most tortuous time of life, namely being a teenager and going through puberty again. Ironically, puberty is something you need to go through before you know how to deal with it and by then it is all too late. However, I don't think a second crack at it would be beneficial or enjoyable in the slightest.

Do you remember how bad it was?! Waking up every morning and finding that spots, zits and blackheads had formed a deadly alliance and they had decided to colonise your face. Clearasil adverts would appear to be insulting, as we all know that using any kind of face scrub would not stop the evil puss filled blemishes appearing. You would stand in front of the mirror, popping them one by one, wiping and then possibly following with a fresh squeeze to get that deep rooted gunk out too. And to top it all off, you could guarantee a real big one would show up in the worst of places just before a big social event, namely square on the forehead or on the tip of your nose. But they weren't the only thing.

Suddenly your smooth skin starts sprouting hair. Now the pubic hair has never been a big problem. Once you're over the initial itchiness and subsequent friskiness that comes with hormones and the such, it then brings a whole new problem. Body odour! Yes, you spent quality time in front of the mirror, draining you face of zit juice, only to find that the hair in your armpits smells like it has been sleeping on the streets of London for 3 weeks. I always wondered if it randomly left my body over night, went for a marathon run to build up a heavy sweat, let itself dry and then re-attach itself. I say that and I am being over dramatic about my situation. I know guys who when they woke up in the morning, well, it had more of a 'scent au sewer' about it. Either way, it required doubly long showers and so it was time consuming and downright nasty if people weren't willing to see the sweat scrubbed through to the point of decent fragance.

Then there was the hormones. Sure it was exciting to have a new crush every week but let's be honest, most came to nothing. They became topic fillers at camping trips and sleep overs. But you would lose total control and be devastated because that girl, who was totally out of your league, suddenly kissed another guy. You would sit there and listen to your poor mate about how he was gutted that he missed the chance you knew he never had. You would comfort him in the knowledge that next month, he would be fancying someone else, leaving out the detail about how you had snogged his original crush anyway because she was easy. (Let's be honest, being easy is true for 90% of teenagers. You've just got to get them snogs on the scoreboard)

This would all come out at a sleepover, whilst you were trapped in the living room of the home of one of your mates. You would be curled up on the sofa, if you were lucky, and if not, on the floor. You would be in for a terrible night's sleep, everyone in the room would end up knowing your secrets and someone would be subject to a cruel practical joke (involving ice cubes... or laxatives... us guys shouldn't be left to our own devices!). At times, they were tantamount to a trip to Hell. It was like a night at Haunted Hill Mansion. You could go home if you made it through the night, without having the lady of the house's make up applied to your face during your slumber. Or maybe if you didn't slap the shaving cream, that was squirted into your hand previously, straight into your face as you wake up. Navy SEALs don't have to endure that kind of torment in training!

Between sleepovers, spots, sweat stench and hormones, puberty is by far the worst time of your life. You have an identity crisis for one. At least at your mid life crisis, you get to go out and buy a sports car or something stupid. In your teenage life crisis, it is eat ice cream until you cry or throw up. The world can end for the smallest social indescretion and life is a daily rollercoaster. I'd rather be tied to a chair in Guantanamo Bay! Teenage life was never a treat; it was torture! Forget being a kid again, it's safer this side of the puberty line

This Is My Status

My brother Josh is a genius. I don't say because we jumped out of the same genetic pool but because it is a fact, not just any simple genius but a comedy genius. He doesn't say much but when he does it is worth hearing. So this one goes out to him because he was the inspiration for it. Reading out the status of people on various social networking websites, the comedy potential is very high. Granted some of these are not of my own but thank you to those that did contribute. You will get no credit, money or glory but at least you can smile and foolishly think that one of these is your work, when really you stole it from someone else. So I offer some of the best status messages you could have with my name as the prefix.

Joel Sparks floats like a butterfly and stings like a Tomahawk missile. At Mach 3! To the face!

Joel Sparks is allowed to talk about Fight Club

Joel Sparks picked his nose and actually found gold

Joel Sparks threw a boomerang and it didn't come back because it was afraid of him

Joel Sparks believes it's not butter... in fact, he knows it's not

Joel Sparks played Russian Roulette with a fully loaded gun... and won!

Joel Sparks isn't in the Bible because God can't afford the copyright

Joel Sparks used his facial stubble to light a match

Joel Sparks would like to be around at the end of the world but he has dinner plans

Joel Sparks thinks going out with someone who is terminally ill should be called an expiry date

Joel Sparks wants to be a big sports star, so he can appear in crappy adverts when he is over 65 to supplement his pension

Joel Sparks is planning on a mid life crisis early so he can get the Ferrari now

Joel Sparks shot J.R

Joel Sparks is not gay but his boyfriend is

Joel Sparks has to type at 50 mph or else his keyboard will blow up. Damn you Dennis Hopper!!

Joel Sparks is a nobody and nobody is perfect.

Joel Sparks thinks it is only funny until someone gets hurt... then it's hilarious!

Joel Sparks is one in a million. That means there is 1000 of me in China

Joel Sparks is tired of women's chests staring at his eyes

Joel Sparks tried sniffing coke once but the ice cubes wouldn't fit

Joel Sparks is busy putting his M&M's into alphabetical order

Joel Sparks can play DVDs with just his finger

Joel Sparks is the Sixth Element

Joel Sparks is due to be the next face on Mount Rushmore

Joel Sparks can get blood out of a stone

Black Is Better

I DON'T GET IT BUT it is a stone cold fact. Black people are genetically cool. I don't care what people say, it is a fact. I have indisputable evidence and to be fair, I think many people will agree with me. It makes me think that racism is no longer spurred on by ignorance but in fact jealousy.

How petty is that! That is the equivalent of spitting on Wayne Rooney's feet because he knows how to kick a ball or Beethoven's hands because the guy knew how to play the piano! If we went on that notion of persecuting people for the genetic talent head starts they were born with, only Paris Hilton and Jim Davidson would currently avoid the mob. And then Paris would be hated for her riches and Jim because he is ginger. Funny that, black people are persecuted because they are superior in so many things and ginger people are slagged because they don't tan, just their freckles join up. Anyways, back to proving my point...

You go to any wedding party and what you get is a dancing display that wouldn't look good in the 80's, never mind today. Everyone is dancing like their dad at a disco and train wrecks don't look that horrific! Yet in amongst it all is a slowly growing circle of women and even a few men. That is right, someone that has got the dances skills to pay any kind of bills and you can bet that they are black. Something happens when they get on a dance floor. Their hips detach and their joints somehow no longer have to apply to the laws of physics, causing the ultimate in sway and shake moves. Dance moves of the highest order are unleashed and suddenly Wade Robson looks like a bouncing muppet next to these guys.

And that is not all. They can pull off ridiculous outfits. I have a colleague at work that frequently turns up to parties in an all white outfit look. Now the ladies drool a river over him and yet any white guy can dress in all black and he blends in with the shadows. P Diddy knew what he was doing when he started throwing his White Party. He must have women throwing themselves at him. Even when I see an ebony lady in ivory colours, I think "Aye Carumba!" It just works.

Get them to sing and they all sound like Usher and Rihanna. Get them to run a race and five World Record breakers show up. Get them to tell a joke and they all become Chris Rock. They just naturally ooze charm and charisma. And do you know why? Because they are just happy being themselves. Talk about loving the skin you're in.

I once said that blonde is not a hair colour, it's a lifestyle. Black is not a skin colour, it's a way of life. And from here, it looks good. Ladies and gentlemen, time to abandon our disco Dad dancing, fashion foolish ways and get some 'chocolate' into our lives. Black is where it's at!

Video Game Your Life

As I walked past a video game store the other day, I realised that the video game era has died down a lot lately. Sure the latest machines and games are coming out but it doesn't feel the same as when war was raging across school playgrounds, namely Nintendo vs. Sega. Those were the days when the only battles that mattered were Sonic vs. Mario, Ken vs. Ryu and Double Dragon vs. Final Fight. I don't know what it was but it seemed like those days were better than the ones we have now. Maybe because so many of us got sucked into that video game world, not as bad as Captain N: The Game Master, but sucked in all the same. It took over our lives to the point that I began to wonder what the world would be like if we lived by video game rules.

I think it would be great. First of all, as long as you saved it, you could always keep coming back to that point that you had been successful and have another crack at it. Granted most guys would then save their lives just before going into a club and then reload time after time until they found the girl that would sleep with them. I know that sounds bad but then think of all the girls that would save their first clothing choice before changing their outfit a dozen times before going back to their original choice. They could just load their life up at that point and we would never have to wait for them ever again!

Disagreements would have to be settled in a slightly more aggressive fashion though. There would be two clear cut options. If it was a dispute between two people, they would have to don ridiculous outfits (we're talking bizarre armour for the boys and bikinis for the girls), learn incomprehensible phrases such as "fight for a gherkin!" and slug it out as soon as some booming voice shouted "FIGHT!" Inevitably it would be a 'best two out of three' contest. If there were 3 or more in the debate, then a death match would be called. All the people involved in the dispute would be dropped in a mystery building, handed one pistol, which somehow could carry 700 bullets and yet only one was needed to kill an opponent. However, just by pressing Start, you could be revived and carry on the shoot out until the 10 minute timer ran out. Most kills wins the argument. Not only would you be able to get your anger and murderous rage out but you could do it without actually killing anyone on a permanent basis. This would be great for everyone except the court system, which would have to close since there was no real crime and civil cases could be solved in a more fun fashion.

There are other benefits. Mushrooms would no longer be dangerous to eat except for the fact they make us double in size. As long as we had change on us, we could run into spikes and other dangers because all it would cause us to do is drop our precious pennies and we could just pick them up quickly again. All natural disasters could be switched off because the mayor does not want that hassle when building his sim city. We could drive our cars and run into walls, traffic and off the road and all it would do was slow us down from 150mph to a sluggish 65mph. And then we could just use our turbo boost to get ourselves back on track. We could take on armies galore by ourselves and when the numbers get too great, just use our special attack to wipe everything out. And whenever you got weak, one piece of food would restore all your energy.

Granted it is all fantasy but there are plenty of cons to the life of a video game. To get the girl of your dreams, you would always have to rescue her from the clutches of an evil villain. To do that, you would have to wade through his personal army first. Then, whenever you have succeeded in something, life would turn around to you and say "Congratulations, now try it in hard mode" like the first time wasn't tough enough! And only when you had done it in hard mode would you unlock the new costume. Talk about tough clothes shopping!! It would be easier just to go with your girlfriend to the High Street!

Video games will never die because sometimes you want to stop being the boring desk job guy and become a super hero with ability to jump stupidly high, shoot fireballs from your fingertips and then jump into a high powered sports car that is invincible with machine guns behind the head lights, then unleash your dance moves on four arrows, show your best guitar moves and sing like a pop star. It's mad, it's sad but it was always a lot of fun!

The Complaint Consequence

Customer service. It is never going to be the strong point of the British nation. We are good at plenty of things but not that and yet we, as a public, are not exactly doing our best to change that. Why? Because we don't like to complain. We like to moan privately but not complain publicly. For most people, this is because we are quite cowardly, not wanting to make a scene. Our complaint will constitute just not going to that place of business again. However, there is far more reason to not complain.

Let me give you a few examples. You go to the hairdressers and they do your hair and then get that poxy little mirror, hold it behind you and ask if that is ok. Now first of all, you can't really see what your hair looks like but even if it doesn't look right, you instantly go "Yeah that's great." Now if you spoke up and said "Well, no it's not what I asked for. Could you manage to get my hairline straight at least?" then you know that after they have fixed it, you're name will be dragged through the gossip mud like only the local snippers can do.

It is the same when you take something back to a shop and they seem reluctant to take it. You know that if you kick up a fuss, the unhelpful maggot on the service desk will just give in with a huff. They will then take that "harrowing" experience up to the staff room at lunch. You will become the topic of conversation and be likened to Hitler, only made out to be worse.

Restaurants hold a special fear for the complaint. You are there, munching away and the food is not good enough. It has happened to all of us and the waiter comes over and asks "Is everything alright?" We instantly smile and say "Yes it's fine" thinking that we'll give no tip and that will suffice. If we told the truth and asked for better food, the chef would take it as a personal insult, prepare a masterpiece and then lace it with his own spit. Now he can argue it helps the flavour but I'll pass on the human fluid as a condiment. So if we stripped it to the bare bones, we should say "This food is terrible, so bad that I would prefer a secondary effort with saliva mixed in, courtesy of your buffoon of a chef!" It might not be popular but it will still yield the same result.

There are serious consequences to complaining but maybe what we need is someone to take a stand, take a few hits on health, reputation and ego and maybe then we'll get the customer service we pay for. And I commend the person who does it... because it sure as hell isn't going to be me!! I like to choose my seasoning for my food!

The Sober Guy

On a night out, there is one thing to fear more than aggressive bouncers, ugly munters who are playing the law of averages by trying it on with everyone and binge drinkers who just seem to spray vomit. That is the sober person. Be it the designated driver or just the guy who doesn't drink, that individual is by far the most powerful person in your party. There are plenty of reasons why you should let the sober guy be present but, be warned, he can be a blessing and a curse all in one.

How do I know this? Because I am the sober guy. So let me give you an insight to the night that I and all other sober guys have when you are getting leathered. First of all, because you are all getting drunk, the crowd euphoria tends to pick the sober guy up and bring the mad party animal out of him. He knows that he can get away with being a maniac with the rest of you because you will not remember most of it anyway. We have a great time but we are still aware enough to be on the lookout for those great comedic moments that can be converted into good quality blackmail material. By the end of the night, we are just as worn out as you are but we won't go home and throw up. And remember, we could actually taste the kebab at the end of the night!

Now the sober guy is the man that saw you dancing with the fat girl on the dance floor and was the only one that seriously considered going over to save you. He inevitably backed up though because he did not want to take your place as the object of Tubby's desire. It is why he does not want to share that drunken hug with you too because the thought of her flab crease perspiration being passed third hand just makes him want to die. However, he is also the first one to whip out his mobile and get digital evidence of the 'train wreck' that is happening on the dance floor. It will be shown around the office or on plenty of websites for all the evening's entourage to examine with gleeful delight.

He is also the one who only almost always gets off with someone hot. Sure there will be the truly dedicated drunkard that has to plant one on the sober guy (and that feels like 'lip rape' when he or she is nasty) but otherwise, it's a hot and horny individual that we get. Chances are that she is a birthday girl or a member of a hen party. Now the sober guy is a great wingman because he will keep encouraging you to have a go for the one you've spotted. The reason for that is, however, that he wants to go and try his luck with the pretty one you haven't spotted. Sober guys spot the girl that is not only hot but so easy that frankly, painting by numbers is a greater challenge.

However, we are not all bad. We are the one that pulls you away from the fight. We are the one that carries you home. We are the one that helps you remember why you had a great night. We are the ones that can tell you where on earth you got that traffic cone. We are the ones who stand as watch guard, as you relieve yourself in a shop doorway. We are the ones that make you laugh about it come a day or two later. You tell us all about how you love us, respect us and look up to us when you're drunk and when we see that raw side of your character, we don't think you're drunken fools. We realise that really, most people are not so bad and that they are worth the air that they breathe. But it is the one time we can get one over you. So be warned!

Shows I Watched as a Kid

MAJOR TV STATIONS ARE NOW deciding that there is no longer a market for children's TV. They say it is because children are not watching anymore because they have other distractions, like specialist channels and the internet. Personally I think the quality of children's TV has dipped so much, that children don't want to watch the rubbish being provided. It makes me sound old, being a child of the 80's and 90's, but things were so much better in our day. We had that early phase of cheap rubbish but then the shows got inventive enough to hide some of the truly terrible bits.

For example, there were many poor art shows until Art Attack came along. Neil Buchanan has to go down as a children's TV legend. Kids around the nation would suddenly see a load of gardening tools and some plastic sheeting and think of how they could use it to make a 30 foot picture of a tractor. Not only did he inspire kids but I'm pretty sure he kept the PVA glue industry going single handedly. Everything he did required you to finish up, and then take a cocktail of 1 part water, 2 parts PVA glue, smothering the art work and then leaving it over night until it was shiny and hard. The only disappointment was The Head made me wonder if any of the statues at a museum would start talking and when I realised that it wouldn't happen, well I was gutted.

Cartoons these days lack imagination. I remember Danger Mouse, a truly legendary show that was exciting for the younger viewer but had the comedy for the older viewer, which was on a par with any other sit com of the day. Captain Planet and the Planeteers actually made fighting against climate change cool before politicians ruined it. Although thinking of all the powers the Planeteers, how gutted would you have been to have got the 'Heart' ring? Your colleagues can shoot fire, cause earthquakes, call on tidal waves and start a tornado. What can you do? Talk to the animals. Oh dear, aren't you special?! And of course, Teenage Mutant Hero Turtles, the essential viewing! Suddenly everyone wanted to be a ninja and eat copious amounts of pizza. They were just better than what the kids have today.

Even the game shows were better. Back then, the adults had to be content with Krypton Factor and Play Your Cards Right. However, we had a ruck of top notch games. The Legend Neil Buchanan brought us Finders Keepers, with the instruction to "raid the room" and of course the contestants would then have to ransack the place. Half the time they wouldn't have needed to because it would promptly explode with ribbons, glitter and balls you get from dodgy ball pools. And the item was always in the wash basket. Why was there a wash basket in the lounge, kitchen and every bedroom? We had Fun House, where no one thought that Pat Sharpe's mullet was ridiculous and every event was some kind of basic challenge that involved 4 gallons of gunge. And of course, the twins. No one knew their names but us boys didn't care; they introduced us to the finer side of puberty.

And of course, there was my personal favourite. Knightmare! That must have been an interesting pitch meeting to sell that idea. Put a kid in a horned helmet and get his three mates to guide him through rooms, picking up random objects (which if they had any sense, they would always pick up the key and leave the ruby behind) and somehow they would always find an apple just as their life force was about to run out. It was essential Friday afternoon viewing. I would be screaming at the screen for them to use the spell or just to run before those goblins actually caught up with them. So much homework didn't get done until last minute and we are thankful to Knightmare for that because seeing if the team could get to level 3 was more important than trigonometry and Shakespeare.

I had a glut of good shows in my childhood. It carried on to my teenage years but that seems to be tailing off rapidly. I was part of the chosen childrens generation of top TV shows, when stuff was adventurous, ridiculous but utterly compulsive viewing. If there is any kind of show that needs resurrecting, it is some of the shows I watched as a kid.

The 13th Day of Christmas

CHRISTMAS... 'TIS THE SEASON TO be jolly... fa la la... hold up... why? Christmas, whether you're a Christian or not, is meant to be a joyous time but lets be honest, is it really that great? Sure, you're thinking about the magic, the lights and the gifts but they are blinding you from an excruciating time that is riddled with stress and over indulgence. If Roy Wood got his wish and it really was Christmas every day, suicide rates would be through the roof! I'm not being a killjoy or a Scrooge type with this. Trust me on this one. You'll be in agreement with me soon enough.

First is the music. The classic Christmas carols are sung and they are all part of the nice traditions but it is the pop songs that are brought out every year that go right through you. They are tiresome, cliche and cheesy. Between Mariah Carey telling us her that all she wants for Christmas is you ("you" referring to which ever rapper she hasn't had yet) and Slade announcing that here Christmas is (like we didn't know!). Christmas music tends to get worse with each passing year and now we know that each year it will be the product of the winner of a reality TV show, it takes all the credibility away. With The Pogues being the last band to release a Christmas song of true genius, it shows how downhill Christmas has gone.

Then you think that it is ok. We still have the gifts. Yes and then you can remember what you went through to get them. In an almost WWE style Royal Rumble, barging your way through mothers that are desperate to spoil their brats at home and the men trying to find a present for their wives that won't be returned on Boxing Day, you try to survive the shopping gauntlet. Inevitably there will be one present, the key present, that will be sold out and will only be available on Ebay for a small country's GDP!

Then there is the films! Oh my goodness, they come at you with that overwhelming sweeping sugary goodness that it makes you want to throw up. Usually they comprise of some magical story about how Santa is real and how everyone comes together at Christmas. Hollywood has redeemed itself at times, before you all think I am having a go at the film studios. After all, the best Christmas movie of all time is clearly Die Hard (it's a Christmas film!) and the Home Alone movies really do make me chuckle. However, too many of them are too twee. And the great thing is how the BBC and ITV advertise the great films they will be showing as big exclusives. Do they not realise that they are years behind and 90% of us have seen those films already and chances are we got it on DVD last Christmas?!

Sure you decorate and it looks pretty but you had to dedicate a day to getting those lights, that tree and tinsel all up. It will take you a whole day to take them down too and that will be a depressing day because Christmas is over and the next day off work is miles away. Yes you get loads of food but the turkey becomes boring and the chocolate becomes sickly and fattening. You get presents that you are grateful for out of instinct and then wonder what people are trying to say when they have all given you aftershave or perfume. You come to realise that you have a better party for New Years than you do for Christmas.

To top it all off, the days are as dreary as an episode of Eastenders, the weather is cold and the roads dangerous. Drink driving goes up and still the chav fuelled Escorts blast around. Let's be honest, we all love the sales that come after Christmas. Once Christmas is over and we assess the damage and tuck into the heavy duty retail therapy, we look back on it fondly but it was, in reality, Hell. So what do I want my true love to give me for Christmas? The 13th day of Christmas... then I know it's all over!!

RAGE

A common fear among us is that of road rage. We worry that some psycho will take advantage of the big lump of metal he is steering and use it against us as a lethal weapon. I am not so convinced. Maybe I am the other side of it, in that I cannot understand how we have so many bad drivers in this country. I get annoyed by people pulling away slowly from traffic lights, people doing 40mph in a 60 mph speed limit and people deciding that they only need to indicate when they are halfway through turning or changing lanes. And while I don't actually do it, the thought of running them off the road does sound awfully appealing. Purely to make the roads a better place though. Ah who am I kidding?! People annoy me and I generally want to make them pay for being insufferable idiotic fools. But I do disagree with the road rage idea... I think rage reaches many facets of life.

We have all had that time where we are walking down a busy street and then there is that stupid person who walks slowly in front of you. They are not looking in the shops, they are not particularly old or infirm. They are just walking slowly, like they are waiting for a gust of wind to pick them up and carry them to their destination. And I'm sure you are like me in that you have wanted to just punch them in the back of the head or grab them and throw them into traffic. What we going to call that? Pedestrian rage? Nonsense! It is rage against stupidity!

There is that person in everyone's life that is overly clingy. With the advances of technology, that clingy nature tends to manifest itself in the form of excessive text messages. Texts were meant for quick info, simple questions, good jokes but not for conversation or a primitive Big Brother system. Yet everyone has had that person that just wants to text over and over. If you could send a text that would result in a fist bursting out of that person's mobile phone that would crack them across their jaw, you would pay the 50p for the VMS (Violence Messaging Service). So what would call this? Text Tantrums? Don't be stupid!

You get angry at the people who make Revels because they keep making the coffee ones. They made an advert about how no one likes them and still they make them! We get angry when we find that someone had put the orange juice carton back in the fridge when it is completely empty. You wonder why the culprit has not learned what a bin is for. We get annoyed with that idiot that seems to think the advert about turning your mobile phone off in the cinema doesn't apply to him. He is a brave soul to be doing that in a film that is encouraging violence and murder because one of these days someone will follow through on the celluloid promptings. And worst of all, we feel that rage against people who just lose their temper because they are having a bad day. What is their problem? If I want to walk slowly, I will WALK SLOWLY!

Rage is empowering, relieving and at times necessary. However, it makes you forget one thing. You forget that, at times, you can be a total plum too! SO CALM DOWN!

Breakdown of the Break Up

FEW PEOPLE HAVE MANAGED TO avoid it and those who have are very lucky indeed. Breaking up with someone is just a horrid experience and not just for the fact that it is the end of a relationship. Think about it. Usually if a break up is happening, then it is not working and the break up is probably for the best. However, it is the excruciating process that you have to go through as part of the build up, execution and aftermath that make it about as much fun as running a rusty blade over your nether regions. Yes it is painful! Hopefully though, I can walk you through it to the point that you just laugh at it and soothe the pain.

Now first of all, a break up does not start with the line "It's not you, it's me" (and in case you were wondering, that line does actually mean "The problem is you and I don't want to work through it"). No, the break up starts much earlier than that. It usually starts with arguments and possibly using the chips of power in the relationship to control the situation, which is rapidly spiraling out of control anyway. The chips of power being fewer gifts and not answering texts for guys and withdrawal physical pleasures and sulking for girls. Admit it, doesn't matter which side of the equation you are, you have done something like that.

You can feel a break up coming on, so you try to rip those cracks open with pointless debates, speculative accusations of your partner being distant or different, or in fact being distant or dismissive. It is like you are trying to edge it even closer to the break up point. Either that or you are trying to get them to do the deed by treating them like rubbish. However, that is where it all starts.

Then comes the break up itself. There are many ways this can be done. The harshest being the text message ranging right down to the nicest being the two hour discussion, locked in a room picking the bones out of it. For some reason, doing it to face to face is considered the most noble but I do not see why. Going to tell a girl why I don't want to be with her to her face does not seem more honourable than just telling her on the phone. At least then she doesn't have to see how serious I am being when I say I'd rather be with a goat than her. Granted, texting a girl with the message "Hey honey, welcome to Dumpsville... population: YOU!" is pretty savage but it is a lot better than telling her "Baby, I'm gay and you made me that way."

Now the various grotesqueries are bad enough when trapped between you and your other half. However, it is usually at this point, the aftermath, where suddenly the two parties feel that having just them involved is not nearly enough. All the close friends have to be drafted in like we are trying to put together a United Nations resolution. A team of 20 people are pulled in to analyse, comfort, mope, moan and ultimate slap you out of depression and into reality. You ask all those stupid questions like "Why did he want to break up with me?" "What did I do wrong?" and the ever so annoying "Why does this always happen to me?"

Yes we know you are hurting and rest assured, we do care about you but we offer soothing words and comfort only so you will shut the hell up! That person does not want to be with you... the only reason you want the relationship to still exist is for you and your happiness, not your previous partner's joy. So get it in your head, sulk and devour a tub of Ben & Jerry's and then move on. We want you to be happy and we want to share in that but we don't want your misery with it as a package deal.

The break up is that time when you become very selfish, very self involved and think the world is against you. Yet it should be a time you come to learn a valuable lesson. When you have someone special, treasure them everyday you are with them because hating them is a set of arguments, a text message and a tub of ice cream away!

I've Got The Power

WE HAVE ALL HAD THE discussion about if we had a superpower, what would it be? No doubt we either instinctively pick the ability of our favourite superhero or we take our time and choose the ability that we think would benefit us the most. For some reason, I worry when people don't answer straight away when I ask them such a question. I wonder what is going through the twisted little mind of the person who is coming up with a solid answer. They have forgotten that it is a trivial question and they have already begun formulating how to use their new found talent!

What do they expect to do with this imaginary power?! You have gained the ability to heal from all injuries and what will you do with that power? Become a parachute tester? Maybe follow in the footsteps of Evel Knievel? Probably because you are a hypochondriac who thinks they have the Bubonic Plague when actually they have a cold. This is the kind of person that wants pity and sympathy delivered in truckloads and when asked if they want a drink, they request a Lemsip as their choice of beverage.

Then is the poor soul who wants to be invisible. You have got to wonder what is going on there. If it's a teenage boy who is ruled by hormones more than intellect, then chances are it is for the opportunity to sneak into the girl's changing room unnoticed. If it is not revealing the pervert of the group, it is the one who is socially inept because they feel like no one notices them and they say it so everyone knows they feel like no one knows they are there. Chances are you will hear them say that and disregard them just as quickly whilst wondering "Where on earth did she come from?"

You can almost guarantee that the one who says super strength goes to the gym too much or got beat up regularly at school. Super strength might seem extremely practical when it comes to superpowers. However, every time someone on your street is moving, you can bet that you will be asked nicely, possibly with the lure of a glass of orange juice, to lift that furniture out of the house and into the moving van. Any time some heavy lifting needs to be done, then all of a sudden, you would be expected to drop everything and skip to it.

Then there is telepathy. How annoying would it be to have a conversation and know what the person is going to say before they say it? It would be like talking to yourself! And then people would be so paranoid of you hearing what they really think of you that you hear them coming up with stuff to fill their minds. Shopping lists, favourite songs, sick jokes and twisted fantasies would come out of the woodwork and pollute your mind faster than the Chernobyl disaster.

The person who wants to fly is probably just lazy. The person who wants to shoot lightning is clearly psycho. The girl who wants to be immortal is vain and the guy who wants to control fire is still a 7 year old child. The reality is that we already have gifts, abilities, powers, call them what you want. I know what mine is and I already use it when I can. I've got the power of being highly intuitive, so what is yours? When you've spotted it, use it and then you won't need to rip off some comic book character. You'll be your very own superhero!

Inside a Blonde's Mind

THERE IS SOMETHING ENTERTAINING YET frustrating about a blonde moment. Mainly the domain of the female of the species, it is bewildering how the educationally superior ladies can have these moments of sheer stupidity. What is happening in their heads? With that said, guys can have them too. It is something that science will never quantify but we could do with some insight on it. Let's be honest, we have all encountered it and felt the pain, as we slapped our hand hard against our forehead. Dare you join me inside the mind of a blonde?

Now a true blonde moment comes from a girl that you think should be quite bright. I know one such girl, a true blonde and I absolutely adore her, who once asked a quiz question "Which country is the War Crimes Court found in?" Now for anyone who doesn't know, it is in The Hague. So I answered "Holland" to which the girl in question said "Wrong". So I sit there, wondering where it could be. I ask for a clue to which she informs me it is more north. So I give up and she says "The Netherlands". Literally everyone around us burst out laughing. Forget that she didn't realise that Holland and The Netherlands were the same place, where did she think Holland was when she said The Netherlands were more northerly?!

Blonde moments tend not to be someone being stupid but someone trying to be clever and the brain misfiring. The blonde in the story above is very intelligent but bless her, she went for something above and beyond her. The brain just shot a blank. The reason guys have less is because we are lazier. We are never operating above our brain power means. In fact, our minds are less efficient than a 5 year old PC with dozens of viruses!

Not only that, it is tricky to have a blonde moment when apparently men think about sex every 7 seconds. Is it just me or does that seem like a waste of the other 6 seconds?

It gets better though. Blonde moments are more powerful when they are more simple. What happens is the mind is going for more complex matters and indeed more matters in general. Suddenly things of simplicity get shoved to that blonde department in the brain and the potential of cringe worthy comedy is huge. Another blonde moment saw a girl I know ask me the question "How do you spell the word 'that'?" I looked stunned at the ease of the question at hand. As I said "T-H-A-T" I wondered if it was a trick question. Then as she looked at me and told me I was so clever, all she heard was my roar of laughter. Insensitive I know but I couldn't contain myself. A blonde moment is based in a smart girl putting a simple thing at the back of her multi-tasking mind.

Now let me tell you one thing I have learned from all of this. I love blondes and I don't mean restricted to hair colour. Women put such effort into life and us men don't. Yet for a brief moment, we catch you up and have a cheap little victory when ladies have a blonde moment. And best of all, you hand it to us. I used to think it would be scary inside a blonde's mind but now I have come to the realisation that really, it is probably one of the most endearing parts of the female soul. Vulnerable, fragile and honest but ultimately... beautiful!

Sleeping With The Accents

Now there is something about the accents the world has to offer. Each is unique and has its own special characteristics. I am a big fan of the Irish accent. I think it is the sexiest accent in the world. If you could sleep with an accent, for me Irish would be it. It got me thinking though, what would the Irish accent be like in bed? I think I would be in for a long, sensual loving night that would probably want to have a heavy booze session afterwards. After I came to that conclusion, it got me going on other accents.

Take, for example, the Welsh accent. It is dirty. Unadulterated filth. Every time you hear a Welsh girl speak, it goes through me a little bit. However, it also sounds like it the kind of accent you would take to bed and a few hours later, you would emerge a total mess and a big smile on your face. I'm talking bruises, scratches and a swollen lip from being bitten too much. It is the accent that is only for a one night stand.

Then there is the French accent. You would be a total slave to that one. It is the accent that will push you to the bed and then tie you to the bed posts with silk scarves. It would have its wicked way with you gently and while it would be very enjoyable, it would be ultimately frustrating. The French accent would be like, well, the French. Very arrogant and think their way is always the best and so it would get boring after a few times. You would end up cheating on the French accent with a Welsh accent and you know it.

Whilst I am jumping through random accents, am I the only one who thinks a Mexican accent would more often than not have a STI and should be avoided like the plague?

Anyway, there is the German accent. My goodness, it sounds like barbed wire being dragged out of their throat! I have no doubt a night with a German accent would involve whips, chains and a gimp mask. It would not be pretty, it would not be enjoyable. It would be savage and you'd come out of it scarred for life. How women like Heidi Klum and Claudia Schiffer came from that nation, I'll never know.

Then there is the Italian accent. It would be romantic, sensual, beautiful... oh who am I kidding? It would take forever. Italians like long operas, slow football and lazy lifestyles. The accent reflects that and you would end up getting bored. You would be in that awkward situation where you would look over and ask "Can we finish now?" In case you are wondering, that's not good. Everyone knows the marathon is the most boring event. The sprint is by far the best!

If we ever got to sleep with the accents, it would turn the whole world around. Mexico would be quarantined or at least run by Durex. France and Italy would no longer be considered cultured or liberal but boring and frigid. Germany would be a large S&M club. Wales would be super horny, so not much change there. But one thing is for sure... I'd be living in Ireland right now, sleeping with that accent!

The High Street Gauntlet

HIGH STREET SHOPPING IS SUPPOSED to be dying out. Retail parks have been blamed with their mass options and low prices. However, I think it is something else. It might be the free parking that they offer or usually the close access to McDonalds for that instant heart attack inducing fast food snack. That may be the more realistic option but consider this. It might just be that people are sick of walking a gauntlet of picketing, busking, protesting and sales that litter our High Streets. It is relentless and ridiculous.

One thing I will say is that you are fair game on a High Street. You have left the sanctity of your castle and ventured into the world. You are now on very public property. What do you find on this public property? Someone who usually can't afford their own private property. A beggar, a homeless person. Most people see this person, pleading for money, and instantly dismiss them. They cite the idea that they will take their money and waste it on things they don't need like alcohol or drugs. I find that very amusing when most of the people who think this will then go and spend their cash on the same thing, come the weekend. I may sound unsympathetic here but haven't homeless people noticed that the begging routine is not that profitable? There they are, begging away and then sleeping in a doorway overnight under the middle page of the Daily Star. Seriously, find a job, turn to a life of crime, go squatting but don't think you are going to crawl out of your hole by doing what has kept you there!

Then you will see the charity worker. You spot them from a mile off. They wear those tabards announcing to the world who they support.

You foolishly think that if you don't look at them, they won't stop you. Then they do! And it is a chirpy student type! Dozens of piercings and tattoos, each one seemingly as pointless as probably they think their degree is, and a hairstyle that would suit an abandoned dog better than a real human being. They give this huge pitch about how we should be saving children in Africa, stop torture in America or plant trees in Brazil. You let them finish and think to yourself "I just passed a homeless guy, who I could see was suffering. I didn't give him 50p... why should I give you £2 a month?" Of course, you could always anger them by asking how much they are getting paid for doing this. They will give the cliché answer of how they need the money because they need to eat. Funny they said that because aren't they trying to help people who can't eat? Maybe they should just ship the Africans over here and have them do charity sales jobs. Two birds with one stone!

If you get past them, then there is the survey guy. They want to ask you some questions, it will only take 5 minutes (which actually means 15 minutes) and you will be entered into a prize draw to win a knock off gold clock. I think this lot have wised up to me though. They know I am one of the types to answer the questions with stupid responses and a dead pan face. They always look at me funny but I never let on that I am messing with them. The last one asked my name, to which I said "Sparks" and she said "Ah that's a nice name" and I said "Yeah it's Japanese". She carries on with other questions like "What would you say your ethnicity is?" to which I say "Pakistani". I even offered "1600 Pennsylvania Avenue" as my address but she will be gutted when the current President of the United States doesn't apply for the latest catalogue.

There are buskers that get louder when you walk by, trying to use volume to bully you into parting with your cash, even though they lack real talent to gain a real contract. There are those annoying people that walk slowly and need to get out of your way. There is the guy who thinks that drawing a massive picture on the street is a good idea when hundreds of people are trying to mill around. There is the guy on a soap box who is telling you that only Jesus can save you, when all you want is 50% savings in the shops. All in all, it is a packed picket line that is waiting for you. Maybe you should stay away, hide in the retail parks and take the easy option but you know what, where is the fun in that?! Run the gauntlet! I dare you!

Cost of a Crush

EVERY ONE OF US HAD a crush on someone. It is really exciting when it happens and suddenly all the world seems bright. Yet somehow, with this new found joy, comes the price of having to try to live up to this impossibly high goal. I remember encountering this beautiful young woman and she was stunning. I could literally list the qualities even now of my last crush. Gorgeous smile, flowing brown hair, cracking body and this wonderfully laid back personality. At the time I wondered what it would take to be worthy of such a lady and sure enough, I found myself trying to be better, just to impress her! How pathetic!

Every person does that. They find different ways to try to improve. You find yourself taking a little longer in the shower, checking that you are not only clean but extra fragrant. No longer is brushing your teeth enough, you now need to take up flossing and buying teeth whitening packs. When it comes to us men, we start to shave more regularly, unless she strikes us the type who loves a rough and ready man, then we start developing designer stubble. We invest in an overpriced razor that allows that 5 o'clock shadow to stay stylish.

We then start watching MTV and Will Smith films to figure out the best way to dress. No longer is the hoodie that is on top in the drawer a sufficient option. We actually find ourselves looking at ourselves in the mirror, checking if the jacket we are wearing works. We start buying more expensive smelly stuff in the hope that the investment will make us more alluring. We even start exercising more (or at least kid ourselves we are by taking out a gym membership) in an effort to be a slim and trim version of ourselves.

Then we busy ourselves with a heavy duty reconnaissance mission, talking to everyone associated with our crush. We gather as much info on what they like and try to find similar interests in music, movies and the like. Frankly the CIA doesn't do as much work in spying on someone. Barring taking out a phone tap and planning a full scale stake out, we wait until we have built not only a detailed profile of the crush but of whom we think they would want in a partner. Once we do that, we then think about trying our luck, only to either bottle it or find that the weeks or months of effort have been a waste because she was snapped up in the mean time.

So what is the cost of having a crush on someone? You become probably a better person and chances are a more dateable person too. However, we do tend to develop a slight stalker streak, if not an excessively anal attention to hygiene and fashion. It's a lot of fun, a lot of heartache, a lot of money down the drain and a lot of other chances ruined. A heavy price maybe but for the one time that it pays off, it is so worth it!

Immaturity: The Great Cliché

MATURITY IS OVER RATED. It would have you do everything properly and by the book. I have no problem with doing things by the book but I do have a problem with a cliché riddled life. When you choose your moments of immaturity, you can find the perfect memory to be carved deep into your psyche. I remember going to a local city centre and using super glue on a fifty pence piece to stick it to the paving stone. Over 20 people walked by and tried to pick it up before some joint smoking hippie came by, produced his flick knife and chiseled it from the street floor. Hilarious and memorable!

Immaturity is only cliché when you are a teenager. I love how teens try to rebel and do stupid stuff, like it makes them stand out. They smoke, drink excessively, smash bus shelters, deface walls and film all their irresponsible activities for Youtube. We do tend to label them all chavs but I think that is harsh. What else do they have to do except fall into the age old clichés of rebellion and stupidity? If we want them to be better behaved, we need to provide them with all the activities that adults have.

Mind you, I don't know if that would work. We give our politicians plenty of problems to solve, plenty of money for the trouble and plenty of privileges. What do they do with this responsibility? They cheat on their spouses with their secretaries, pilfer money from various illicit means, break promises and then when it all goes wrong, go and have a muck around back home. Casual sex, theft, dishonesty, rebellion and cowardice...hang on; did we elect a cadre of chavs to the Commons?

Well at least the other examples of the mature society fare better surely. Well no actually. Footballers moan about having to play 60 games a year and only being paid a couple million to do it. Minimal work and wanting mega bucks... chavalicious! It reeks of gross immaturity. The same with music and movie stars. They will charge exorbitant fees, of which they deserve very little, and then demand extras on top. It is like a teenager getting dole and then asking for cigarettes on the side. At least they are grown up enough to go get their own!

It really doesn't bode well. Night clubs are now providing for over 30's, the type of people that should have settled down and started a family but no. They are still going out, the men with their grey hair and wrinkles and the women with their excessive make up and chicken wings flapping under their arms. Don't they know that 3am is not a proper bed time? They should leave the 18 - 30 age groups to be the reckless lot and go home and grow up!

It is sad to say it but the biggest cliché in our world is that of immature behaviour. Everyone does it because it seems fun but with everyone doing it for most of their lives, it has become the biggest cliché in our modern society.

Day of the Devil

No one likes Mondays. Garfield the cat declared it as the one day he truly hated. Everything seems to go wrong on a Monday. If Sunday is the Lord's Day, the devil didn't waste anytime claiming the following one! We all have rough days and they are not always on a Monday but it does feel like the worst day of them all. The weekend is over and you are as far away from the next weekend as you can be. The full working week is ahead of you and it is doom and gloom through and through.

Your alarm goes off on a Monday and no matter what sound the alarm makes, it is clearly mocking you. It is taking delight in the end of your lie ins and days of leisure. You drag yourself out of bed and need to rush but you don't have the energy to muster any urgency. You have sleep hair (how does it get that messy?). Bad breath from the kebabs or curries of the weekend that could melt metal and that smell of death from your body partying all through Saturday and slobbing all through Sunday. It is the kind of lethargy that makes you feel like getting up feel like you are taking on a Spartan army single handedly. With a spoon.

Then you manage to drag yourself into work (for students this will not really count because they barely surface until Wednesday afternoon). You have the big pile of left over work from Friday. It seemed ok to just dump it there because the weekend was here! It would be ok on Monday. So why does it seem to breed and multiply over those few days and get worse? Your inbox is bulging! You find post it notes on your computer screen and a dozen voicemails on your work phone. You haven't even sat down and already the evils of a Monday have swamped you!

And there is no escape from it. Of course, we have the Bank Holiday Monday. Surely that must redeem the wretched weekday in some way. But no! You see, the illusion is that it is a day off. What it actually becomes is either a day to lock yourself in your house and watch the rubbish films put on TV or dare to venture out to go shopping or to the park or beach. The shopping is like walking right into the middle of a WWE Royal Rumble match. The trip to somewhere to relax is the human equivalent of jumping into a bucket of crabs. And then there are the roads, which will be inevitably clogged up by all the caravans returning to the driveways of their traffic jamming owners. Back from their "long weekend" break in their tin can on wheels. So even Bank Holiday Monday is stressful and not enjoyable.

Monday is the day of the devil. It really has limited to no redeeming qualities. You just want it to end because at least in the other days of the week, there are things worth seeing or doing. If not, at least it is getting closer to the weekend. You just feel too disgruntled with Monday to really get mad at Thursday or any other random day. If we should thank God it's Friday, let's blame Satan is Monday!

10 Lessons from Cartoons

1. ACME are the only company in the world that trade in faulty death traps and gadgets, designed to catch rapid moving animals but ultimately serve to torture to the client who bought the goods. My bet is that Wile E. Coyote keeps all his receipts and that is how he keeps getting more machines. Obviously ACME doesn't offer refunds, only replacement machines.

2. Ducks are stupid.

3. Mice can dodge the pursuing cats better than OJ Simpson can avoid the police. I have no doubt that if Tom was being assisted by the LAPD and a CNN press helicopter with cameras rolling, Jerry would still find some cunning way to avoid capture and being devoured. Then he would hold out in his hole until the heat died down and fresh cheese was there to be eaten.

4. Human and animals can converse in English and if Jessica Rabbit is to be believed, bestiality is ok if the animal in question can make you laugh. A good sense of humour really is the thing a lady looks for!

5. Animals can walk around comfortably in just their fur but if they hop out of the shower, they still need to wear a towel.

6. Yosemite Sam has the only two guns in the Universe with unlimited bullets.

7. Bombs can only go off if the character that lit the fuse is within the blast radius. Obviously suicide bombers got their training from too much Looney Tunes.

8. You don't need pockets. Just reach behind your back and you can produce any kind of required item, mainly placards on a pole that issue an instant gag to the reader.

9. Cats are also stupid.

10. The best thing that cartoons teach is that no matter what, the good guy always wins. In a world that is falling apart, the cartoon world that is labeled as promoting violence actually teaches that right will have its day. In fact, it will have it with a good laugh and within a 5 minute showing time. What more could you want?

The Ex

THERE ARE PLENTY OF UNBEARABLE people in the world. People who talk during the film in cinemas, the French and those who laugh so loud in a restaurant that your table shakes, you know the sort. However, everyone has one person that falls into their undesirable category with the consistent title of "the Ex". Unless you are extremely lucky and found "The One" in your first relationship or been a hermit, locked away in a garage playing random fantasy games, you have an ex. However, the reason your ex drives you to despair may vary.

It could be that they are way too clingy. You have been with them for a little while and suddenly the commitment being demanded gets cranked up at an excessive rate. Suddenly you feel that binding feeling. Your partner is talking about naming babies, meeting your parents and suggesting a trip to IKEA for your next date to pick out curtains. Nothing quite like someone who plans your life for you to make you want to ditch them. However, then when the relationship is over, they go up another gear in an effort to win you back. It is lost on them that what caused the break up will not heal the same wound. You get lavished with more tacky gifts. Your instant messenger buckles under the weight of all their conversational begging for you to take them back. You eventually hit that point where you just scream at them until they leave you alone. It is about as close as us non-celebrities get to having a stalker!

Then they could turn nasty. Now the reasons for a break up are varied. However, it is rare that one side of the break up doesn't feel cheated. The cheated party then takes it upon themselves to breed an air of tension so thick, you need a machete to cut through it. It usually comes in snide little remarks to your face or murmuring and gossiping behind your back. By the time your ex has finished, the world thinks you were cheating with a dozen different people or that you broke up because your partner was getting fat. They just drag you through the mire. It becomes a display of just how childish can your ex become. Let me tell you, the way not to inform your ex that they are being childish is buying them a dummy. It only baits them.

And then there is the ex that feels it is now a contest. Every time they are in the same place as you, they show up with someone and are all over them like fake bling on a chav. You would tell them to get a room but you (and probably everyone else) know that it is purely for show. The victim that your ex is using will be dropped quicker than A level French. They find some fresh meat for the next party and keep going, whoring themselves about in an effort to show that they don't need you. Why they need to provide some kind of confirmation, I have no idea! Maybe they just realise that they can't do as good as you but chances are they never will again. Unless the law of averages is true and since they are going through people like Mariah Carey goes through rapper lovers, they may get lucky. Who knows? Who cares?! You just wish they would get out of your sight!

Some people get lucky and are on good terms with their ex. However, it is the risk you take with the joys of a relationship, that one day this wonderful human being, who inspires all those exciting emotions in you, will one day turn into this unbearable monster that will be a bigger stain on your life than a criminal record. Of all the people in the world you don't want to be locked in a room with, the ex with their jealous, malicious or stalker mentality is one that has to be high on the list to be avoided. The ex... Putting the ex into "EXtra grief!"

List of 5

THE TV SHOW "FRIENDS" HAS a lot to answer for. Apart from giving me years of top quality entertainment and laughs, they have managed to introduce things into pop culture that still exist today. One of those things is the List of 5. The 5 people you could cheat on your partner with. It became a topic of discussion around tables in pubs and between partners over dinner. You have to think out your list carefully before you come to laminate it though. That could be awkward if you don't get it right. So what should you be looking for on your List of 5?

Top of the bill should be your dream partner in everyway. If you are going to show this to your current partner, the top name will catch their attention first. It will say a lot about you and what you look for. We are talking incredible looks, a personality you would go for and hopefully filthy rich too. If you are going to run off with your dream person, you might as well be doing it swimming in money like Scrooge McDuck in Ducktales.

Next one is where it gets interesting. Number 2 on the list should be someone that is a pure lust option. You don't want to have kids with them. You don't want to have dinner with them. In fact, you won't stay the night. Once you've had your fun, you'll call a taxi and be off about 3am. It sounds awfully crude but anyone who denies it will be kidding themselves. There is one celebrity we look at that has a personality and talent that is a bitter disappointment but you just want to have one wild night with them and then never talk of it again.

Number 3 is the trophy. The one you take to parties and you would want all your mates seeing you with. You don't care if she is a rubbish kisser or has a personality that makes watching paint dry an appealing prospect. It is the person you want to go to film premieres with and be photographed next to. You'll stick that photo in the hallway so people spot it first thing as they walk in.

Number 4 is the parent pleaser. Everyone should have someone on their list that is not only hot but one you could take home to the parents and introduce them. Parents worry about their kids but nothing puts their mind at ease quite like their child bringing home someone "nice". So chances are it might be someone who they will know, who will be maybe be a little more homogenised. Basically you would find them on early evening BBC TV and not on late night channel Five.

The final entry is the wildcard. The one that should be so off the page that everyone looks at it and goes "what?" and you reveal a little bit about yourself. Basically it should be that embarrassing crush you have. The one that you will find a lot of people probably share but dare not admit it. For women it used to be Richard Hammond of Top Gear fame and for guys it was... well we have no shame!

The List of 5 is just a bit of fun but when people are taking to laminating it, then you know that some serious thought is being given to it. Yeah it's fun but it says something about your taste. So choose how you will. Be it with caution or abandon, it will tell the world a little bit about you. Are you sure that you want us to know that?

Wedding Day Woe

OH THE DELIGHT THAT IS the Wedding Day. I don't care if you have it planned with military precision; it is a day full of event, disaster, stress, highs and lows, joy and despair. I have been to enough, in fact too many, to be well versed in the event. I've been an on-looker, an Usher and a Best Man on several occasions. Anyone who has been involved in the planning and execution of a wedding day generally wants to be executed at some point in the process. It is a minefield of misery!

It usually starts with the parents of one or both of the engaged people meddling in the proceedings. Now in case they forgot, it is not their big day but they inevitably try to hijack it quicker than Al-Qaeda on an airplane. I imagine it is done just as aggressively too. They storm in with their grand designs, how everything should go and look. The most common thing they do is inflate the day with stuff the bride and groom don't want. The quiet party at the end turns into the Brits, the small guest list turns into the phone book and the bill starts to look more like the budget deficit of a third world country. Parents want the best for their kids and yet somehow end up playing out their own fantasy, waving the financial contribution they are making as their baton of authority. Get them to the wedding and the mother is wearing a ridiculous hat that is matched only in its stupidity by that "I'm being dragged" look the father has on his face.

Then there are the bridesmaids and the Best Man. It is rare, if ever, that a wedding goes by where one or more of the bridesmaids don't complain about the dress they have to wear. It may not be the right colour, size or whatever. Somehow they get so thrilled about being involved and then get into a panic that people will be looking at them. I don't know why they care. The only people that will look that keenly at them are single men, looking to bed them because all this wedding talk has made them desperate. And the Best Man is usually a liability from the off. It is almost like an unwritten law where the Best Man makes a scene of himself and if not, he makes a humiliation of the Groom. Granted that is in his mandate. The Best Man speech should be the most entertaining part of the day. It ends up being cringe worthy, so much so that you can see why God invented snipers.

And then finally, there is the general congregation. Sure there are some good people in there but there are also plenty of idiots. The kind that can't get there in time, even taking into account the bride showing up an hour late! The ones who can't follow simple directions of the photographer if they were handed a sat nav and you can't get them to move, even at gunpoint! There is one who has the screaming kid at the back but they can't go outside with the child. No because we can't hear your toddlers wailing because you are stood near the door! Get out!

Marriage is wonderful, weddings are woe! I hate them and trust me, I personally have been to way too many. No matter how many times it is described as a joyous occasion, it is all too often an annoying and draining experience. Maybe the lure of the wedding night is enough to drag any sorry soul through it all. It is a good job that the couple in question love each other. It will get them through the day and hopefully maybe the rest of their lives together. To the bride and groom!

Practical Joke Perpetrator

THE VICTIM HATES THEM BUT the perpetrator loves them and brags about them, namely practical jokes. I personally love them and I think a well executed practical joke is worth bragging about. In fact this is what I intend to do now by sharing with the reading world some of my most mischievous endeavours, armed with whatever was in the house or in the local store. For the record, some of these may seem illegal but I can assure you, apart from this confession, all evidence of the event is inadmissible.

To give you an idea of what I am capable of, let me tell you what happened when one of my friends and work colleagues foolishly gave me the keys to her place to drop some stuff off. In I went with the practical joke equivalent of carte blanche and I tell you I took full advantage! She was sharing with another girl and so I switched the cereals into different boxes, put green food colouring into their milk, I pushed spaghetti inside their toothpaste, put rice and sugar in their beds, squirted whipped cream in their shoes and turned all the pictures and furniture upside down. They were not impressed! They did try to bring a war upon myself and my fellow flat mates. Did that stop us? No chance!

We then set out a new plan. We went out and bought some Camembert cheese, which is pretty strong smelling stuff, only to go and leave it out on the balcony for four days exposed to the warm summer air. It made you want to wretch in the fresh air, so imagine how bad it was when we posted it through their letterbox. Word is the neighbours considered calling the police after they thought they could smell a dead body. I had this vision of these two girls desperately trying to explain to the police that the only fatality was a block of French cheese.

They thought that would be the end of it but oh no! I wasn't done. So after one of my colleagues assures me that he is proficient with a lock pick (and worryingly he was... he could pick any lock in 90 seconds), we set out to their flat, entered and began filling the bath. Now I know what you are thinking; we filled the bath and left it running all day until they got back. Well we stopped once it was full because then we could put the goldfish in and how at home they looked. So we left them as not just a practical joke but a pleasant surprise. I called them up that night and waited for the reaction, which didn't come until I heard a shrill scream from the other side of the flat. After some calming down and catching of breath, one of the girls picked up the phone and explained how the plug has been broke for the last month and it means the water slowly drains out of the bath. Yes the goldfish were dead! I was crushed, since I did name one of them after me but the screaming and hilarity that had ensued did at least make sure that Sparky's sacrifice was not in vain.

There was the time with the industrial strength chocolate laxatives that lead to one man's trip to the toilet sounding more like a visit to Niagara Falls. Or the time that my car was covered in shaving foam and silly string and even cling film (to be fair my car seems to be victimised more than me). Of course there was the age old "putting make up on a friend's face whilst they were asleep." They were all great and all worth trying out for a laugh. When it comes to practical jokes, make sure you are the villain and not the victim. That way, it will always be funny.

The Real Punch Lines

Jokes are simple. Too simple. They rely on the quick wit and superficial play on words to get a cheap laugh out of the statement. I love them and find it easy to laugh at all of them and we all should. The real thought out answers to some of the simplest jokes are quite complex. They may well provoke the thought "That's not funny but true". Here are the real punch lines.

1. Why did the chicken cross the road? Clearly this is behaviour unbecoming of a chicken and therefore the chicken should be arrested without evidence and held for a month. The chicken should be subjected to intense cross examination, then be plucked, covered in a tangy BBQ sauce and cooked until a confession is extracted. We cannot allow to poultry to go along freely in this world! We need to question everyone's motives!

2. What do you get if you cross a sheep with a kangaroo? The latest in a line of fast food restaurant burgers. The skins and fur of the newly produced flock will work their way to the worst sweatshop in China and be produced as high quality goods, sold in half price sales on the High Streets of our beloved nation.

3. Knock, knock. Who's there? Doctor… didn't you read the sign that says no hawking, salesmen, religions, picketing or surveys? Actually in this day and age, why is someone coming to knock on my door to bother me? It might be Doctor Who or an interrupting sheep but surely they should get with the times and just have a pop up

advert on the internet, if they want to invade my privacy. These joke characters really should learn.

4. What is black and white and red all over? In all likelihood, another American classroom's chalkboard, with the blood of a 'Columbine' style incident on it. A nation that has prided itself on the right to bear arms is now turning into a kiddies killing spree. For a nation that states that the constitutional privilege to own a gun is part of its power to protect itself, it is amazing how they are self destructing so quickly. When their own children are killing each other, who needs terrorists?

5. What do you call a deer with no eyes? The latest and finest example of art. The critics will circle the poor animal and look for the deeper meaning, while the poor deer would just like to be able to look. The media will broadcast and publicise it, the work e-mail inboxes will be inundated with protests about it and yet it will pass by without any major incident. So to gain the same notoriety, the deer's legs will be removed and the "Still no idea" exhibit will become the new controversial Turner Prize candidate.

Thank goodness we can take the simple answers and laugh at them. The reality is that if we didn't poke fun at the world, we would realise how dark it has become. We might as well find the humour in this world; stop being a sour puss and chuckle away. Keep those punch lines coming!

Keep It Short

The world of Instant Messaging Services (i.e. MSN, Yahoo, AOL) has made communication around the world far easier. Yet we have taken it upon ourselves to try and make it that tiny bit quicker with abbreviations for a phrase. Yet they have a face value meaning and over time, they have come to mean something else on a deeper, more cynical level. Here is the Sparks analysis of what people mean when they keep it short.

LOL:- I'm not laughing. I just can't think of anything to say

BRB: - I don't want to talk to you at the moment and I can't be bothered to block you!

LMAO: - That was quite funny

CBB: - This is how I always feel

Excessive use of exclamation marks: - I'm trying my best to seem interesting

TTYL: - When no one else more interesting is online, then I might talk to you

BBL: - Find someone else to talk to

How r u? : - I don't want to know, it is just a typing habit

I'm ok:- I am miserable but I don't want to talk about (actually I do, so nag me and let me wallow in my misery)

X: - A girl's way of saying "Please don't IM me anymore, I'm signing off and I am saying goodbye to a billion people"

Have u got a webcam? : - I want you to get naked for me on camera

Who r u again?:- I have 300 contacts and you are in my Others (I don't care about these people) Group

By abbreviating what we are saying, we are also trying to sneakily hide what we are really thinking. Why? Because we stupidly think the rest of the world cannot handle honesty, when in reality we just want to appear more acceptable to the world. It is us who cannot handle honesty. Keeping it short is about hiding the truth of your cynical soul from yourself.

The Power of the Insult III

THERE IS THIS GROWING TREND in the entertainment world where an original and a solitary sequel are not enough. You have to make a trilogy at least. You insist that is how it was always meant to be and then when times get hard and money is tight, you churn out a fourth entry because needs must. As for insults, I think they go way beyond trilogies or even quadrilogies. They are part of an epic saga, a franchise that runs forever. So here is entry number three in the horror that is "The Power of the Insult".

- Don't stand outside too long. The dustbin men are doing their rounds and they will take you away.

- A face like that deserves an 18 certificate

- What's that smell? Wait… it's all the crap that's coming out of your mouth!

- I'd rather share a bath with a leper than be in the same room as you

- If you end up in Heaven, I won't sell my soul to Satan. I'll offer it for free with extras!

- You've been in a relationship for quite some time now. That must have cost you a fortune in rohypnol!

- It's a good job you've got a short name because you are not bright enough to handle big words

- The height of your career potential is checking that the dole system is still paying out

- I'd rather listen to my own funeral music than you going on

- Your personality makes watching paint dry an appealing prospect

- Promise me that you won't breed. Actually wait… no one is that stupid to help you in that twisted endeavour

- He was huge as a kid too! If someone had stolen his lunch money at school, they could have cleared third world debt with it!

The Dating Inquisition

I HAVE BEEN TOLD MANY times that I am a picky man when it comes to women. In fact, I get analysed a great deal by friends and family in my love life. It is frankly laughable. You may or may not be on the end of such an annoying inquisition through your daily life too. If not, count yourself lucky. It feels like going into the field of battle, trying to dodge the bullets of ignorance and the bombs of "good intentions" mixed with "utter stupidity". You do get a raft of fairly consistent statements and questions thrown at you, just because you are getting of a certain age and are single. Well I am well versed in this from painful personal experience. Let me tell you, it does make you want to carry a shotgun around! So when you get those very irritating lines thrown at you, these are the classic comebacks that you will need. The person will then know that they should at least keep their mouth shut and if not, they will be so offended that they won't talk to you again. Either way, a great deal!

When are you going to find yourself a girl/boyfriend? Well I was hoping you could tell me where you bought yours from, since I'm looking for something cheap.

You know what your problem is. You're too picky. You know you're right, I should just look out for a desperate ugly munter like you did (you can always drop the "did" at the end if they are also single or you like their partner).

Looks aren't everything. Yes but your parents had to tell you that.

You need to be more in touch with your feelings and emotions. I am perfectly in touch with my feelings and emotions. Right now, murderous rage is building up quite nicely to the boil. Would you like to see it in action?

You can't expect perfection. Funny you say that because it seems like you expect me to be perfect. Coming from a flawed fool like you, that is downright moronic.

Why don't you try something new? Expand your horizons like I did? No thank you, I don't want to buy rohypnol off you, it's against my morals.

You don't need to be attracted to someone first. You can learn to love them. Isn't that the motto of a stalker?!

Do you want to be single for the rest of your life? As opposed to being married to a whinger like you?

Some of them are savage but they are always warranted. When people feel like they should get involved in this part of your life, they deserve to be shut out like they are trespassing in Buckingham Palace. Dragged out in front of the masses, tried, convicted and summarily executed. Maybe then we would have the adequate deterrent for those who lead this dating inquisition to the misery of my and many other souls in the world today.

Odd One Out

No matter what they do in the world, there is always an odd one out. A black sheep, someone or something that just doesn't go with the rest. That does seem to be the law of the Universe but I want to know who or what decides to put these peculiar things among its fairly liked peers. Confused? Let me enlighten you with some practical examples.

Let's take Revels, the bag of chocolates. Everyone sits there and enjoys the malteaser, the minstrel and then all of a sudden, you get the coffee one. Who in their right mind wants a coffee chocolate? Chances are you throw it in your mouth in the middle of a cinema screen and so you are unable to just spit it out in a nearby bin. You have to chew it down quickly, with that tortured look on your face. Revels are not the only one. With Celebrations, it's the Bounty. With Roses, it's the Brazilian Darkness. Why do the confectionery gods decide to pleasure us for 90% of the deal and then leave that kick in there?!

Now you are playing a board game. There is always the same routine to start a board game. The quick scramble to get the good playing pieces. When you play Monopoly, people always want to be the car, battleship and the hat. No one but no one wants to be stuck with the iron as their piece. You are playing a game about property and money and you don't want to be stuck with the playing token that makes you look domesticated. If it's Cluedo, the same rule applies. No one wants to be Mrs. White. The sultry Miss Scarlet or the authoritative Colonel Mustard are worthy efforts but the fat old cook? Not an option really!

Another odd one out that springs to mind is when you take a trip to McDonalds. You look up at a menu which offers the standard selections and pick what you have had the last fifty times. However, I have to ask… who orders a Fillet-o-fish? It has been on the menu long enough to make you think its existence must be warranted by adequate sales. To who?! They glue 3 fish fingers together, put the processed cheese slice on top, along with tartar sauce! That is as nasty, if not worse, than putting pineapple on a pizza.

There is one that spawned its peers by its very existence but now is the biggest non-event of what should be a thrill seeking time. You go to Alton Towers and it is stacked with enthralling rides. Nemesis, Air, Oblivion and Rita: Queen of Speed all jump to mind. Yet there is one that is listed as a rollercoaster, therefore by definition should be exciting but offers the same exhilaration as the monorail… the Corkscrew! The last time I went on that dinosaur of a ride, I did remark that I could get out and walk faster. It would be more exciting if it broke down halfway through!

Whoever comes up with these things we call the "odd one out" deserves to be shot. They must be some masochistic freak, trying to find some familiarity in the increased number of failures he can implement in the world. If they are ever let out of the closets they are hopefully entombed in, they are to be avoided. Just like the coffee one in a pack of Revels!

Gaseous Maximus

Now I am never one to skirt around the controversial or the crude. In fact, I take it head on. So let me tell you, I take the issue of farting with no fear or restraint. After all, it is an activity where restraint is removed and we just unleash a vile human function that is laced with huge comic potential. If you think discussion of such a topic is unbecoming, I suggest you move on quick. This will get messy!

No doubt that there seems to be a divide among the sexes on this issue. My father, in his infinite wisdom, taught me that the one thing marriage teaches you is that women fart and it is not perfumed. Women do seem to be very coy about it. If one should ever leave their body, they instantly look blankly at you, like it never happened. Either that or they accuse someone else. Men, we get in there as fast as possible to claim the credit for our work. It is like we carefully chiselled out a sculpture of flatulation akin to the Venus De Milo and we want our acknowledgement. Women look at the farter with disgust, possibly with a tiny snigger. The men sample it quickly so they can give a full review and star rating.

The irony is that I find that women's farts smell worse than men's! Men have a variety of smells. It is highly dependent on how much protein shakes we are having and whether what we had to eat last night was kebab, curry or chinese. Needless to say, we will lift one leg and try to get the best sound we can. The louder, the better, as long as it's not wet sounding. If that happens, you have to make a bolt for the toilet and the emergency wipe is needed. We then pretend to clump part of the smell in snowball form and offer it to our friend's faces. What is weird is that even though you can't do that with smells, they still react like you are holding a ball of fart gas.

Women don't do such things and frankly it comes as a relief. When a woman farts, it is the smell of death. If you were in the room, your eyes water and your flesh starts to melt off your bones. If you weren't and you try to walk in, you walk into an invisible brick wall of 'gaseous maximus'. I don't know where they get it from!

Also, whilst I am on the topic of farting, whose bright idea was it to try and light a fart? Someone realised that it was methane streaming out of our backsides and thought this was a good chance to start a fire. Fine but I have seen many a people try to light them and the flame could be yellow, blue and even green. What have those people eaten to be shooting green flames off their intestinal fumes?!

Farting is funny. I don't care if you are a prude about it, when someone rips one in the appropriate setting, it is hilarious. Avoid a follow through and you are a champion. Sure you will get a few disgusting retorts but farting is like yawning or coughing. As soon as one person does it, everyone starts doing it. Be a trendsetter and drop one of your own 'gaseous maximus' before anyone else does.

We Are Kidding Ourselves

You know, we are a stupid bunch. We seem to think we have that quick solution to everything when, in reality, we are just kidding ourselves. We see something and then we want to project another thing. Why is it that we can't accept a simple error on our part and just learn from it? Why do we have to cover up our true feelings in fear of the consequences? Because, like I said, we are kidding ourselves.

The classic one was when you were a kid and had a juicy scab developing somewhere, chances are your knee or elbow from falling over. It would be well on its way to healing and it would start to itch. You see the white part develop around the edge and it feels loose, so you pick it until it comes off. As you do that, you start to bleed and what do you do? You try to push the scab back! Rather than admit defeat and start afresh, you try to glue it back using your own blood! That won't make it heal quicker; it will just make it a scab topped with dead scab.

Another one that bewilders me is the burnt toast example. Not everyone is as stupid as this but when in a rush, some people burn their toast and don't have time to do another batch. So in an effort to make the toast viable as a breakfast, they just put more butter and marmalade on it. They do this until it is caked in the stuff, so much so that the charcoal toast becomes the topping to the huge wedge of preserve and butter. It is the culinary equivalent of sweeping it under the rug; it is utterly moronic. If there was a fire in your house, you wouldn't put up five sets of curtains to hide the burn marks and take that as acceptable.

There are plenty of other stupid things we do that are motivated by no common sense whatsoever. We get a broken car window and it seems perfectly acceptable to replace it with duct tape and a binbag. Yeah that's brilliant! Lousy security, excessive air conditioning combined with no view.

We watch our national sportsmen or women fail miserably at an event and then describe them as heroes. You're not a hero if you lose the war! And then we watch talent shows where we have been made to watch an excruciating performance by some pleb off the street. Then when a Simon Cowell figure speaks the mind of the nation and tells them how bad it is, we boo the judge! We didn't like them when they were performing, why are we trying to hide that disgust now?

Sometimes you just have to stop kidding yourself and just accept it's rubbish. Life isn't fair. Good tasting food is fattening. Great books are long and have small text. Memorable films come along rarely and it is going to take several trips to the cinema before you find one. And someone genuinely worth spending your life with is the wait of a lifetime. The only comfort you can have is that we are all in this mess together. So let's do it with a laugh and smile!

If The World Was Going To End

It is a question that we ask every now and then, maybe since time began but more recently because of the terror edged world we live in. It is the question "What would you do if the world was going to end tomorrow?" and no doubt we all have different answers, depending on our situation. Well, you probably haven't seriously contemplated the answers. Maybe because you don't want to think that it may happen but let's discuss this and that way avoid the panic during an impending apocalypse. The options abound but here are the merits and down sides to each possibility.

You could go and tell all your loved ones how you really feel about them. Now that might mean telling someone you don't like why you dislike them and just spilling out your disgust and rage in one go. The world is ending and so other people might as well feel like theirs just did. The flipside is telling people you care about that you love them. It would make the whole statement decidedly cheap and forced. You might get away with it because the other person is about to die too. But if you struggle to tell someone that you love everyday that you care, then informing them before their inevitable demise is about as valuable as a second hand condom. So you might want to re-think that answer.

The slightly related response, if not very crude, is to sleep with the next good looking person that was up for it. Now if being promiscuous is your thing, then why are you suddenly waiting for Armageddon to roll around? Not only does it prove you are hopeless as a player, relying on desperation in its ultimate form but also that you are unbelievably shallow. However, how bad would you feel if you asked for sex before someone was about to die and they turned you down? Eternal celibacy was preferred to a night of passion with you. Oh dear. Look on the bright side; you'll have less than 24 hours to moan about it.

Some say that they would have their favourite meal, watch their favourite film or do their favourite activity before it all ends. Not to put a damper on things but the fact that this has been brought on by the end of the world means none of those things would be enjoyable. The food would be tasteless, the film would be a waste of two hours and your favourite activity probably would not be available due to pandemonium.

The only real answer is that you would PANIC! And then see what kind of monster would come out; it would be one of those times you would see your raw real self and it may shock you, maybe impress you. However, you wouldn't get a long to look at it and you should be grateful. You might find yourself to be a shallow, selfish character. The only people who won't panic are the best of us; those who have made peace with their God and, more importantly, themselves. To them, the Apocalypse would be the full stop on a very complete sentence and they are the people I envy the most.

10 Lessons from Music

1. Walking slowly down a hall is actually quite a lung busting speed, since it is faster than a cannonball. Be warned and only do it if you are in supreme physical condition. (Champagne Supernova by Oasis)

2. Britney Spears would like to state for the record that striking young girls or indeed anyone is not acceptable. (Baby Hit Me One More Time by Britney Spears)

3. The only road that is more fun to drive on than the Autobahn and Nurburgring is the road that leads to that fiery pit, owned by The Devil himself. There are no stop signs and no speed limits, so hurtle your way down it! (Highway To Hell by AC/DC)

4. Craig David insists that he wants one week to seduce a woman but will manage it by day 3. Sting, on the other hand, would put it off until the 6th day, knowing that Sunday would be too late. (7 Days by Craig David and 7 Days by Sting)

5. Everything in this world seems to be broken. OK maybe not everything but when it comes to broken things, hearts and dreams are broken in abundance. However, this doesn't mean we should give up. Let's be honest, if there is one good reason to leave, then there will be ten good reasons to stay. (Too Many Broken Hearts by Jason Donovan)

6. Love can be an extremely painful emotion, to the point it can cut you open and leave you dripping blood. To be honest, you'd think someone like Leona Lewis is beautiful enough to find a far more comfortable option in relationships. (Bleeding Love by Leona Lewis)

7. The important thing to look for in a woman is to make sure she has the right vibe. You'd think it was hard to find but apparently Joann, Theresa, Betty, Chip, Gail and a host of others have it. No wonder R Kelly can't control himself. (She's Got That Vibe by R Kelly)

8. If you need a good clean, a good meal and do whatever you feel, whether that be dress up like an Indian or see about joining the Navy, the Young Men's Christian Association is the place you can go, which is a short walk up the street. Just look for the building with four people from a wedding disco standing in letter shape, spelling the acronym. (YMCA by The Village People)

9. Hotsteppers, lyrical gangsters and mister officers are all murderers. Well, they are being accused of it. (Here Comes The Hotstepper by Ini Kamoze)

10. True love is about committing to be someone's dream, wish, fantasy, in fact, everything they need. It is a commitment that should last until the sky falls down on you. Trust me on this one, that is not going to happen for a very long time and whilst it is taught in a song that should be wrapped in Cheddar, it is still true. (Truly, Madly, Deeply by Savage Garden)

49 Things We've Learned

1. Because of the internet, the Numa Numa guy has gone from being that kid who gets bullied at school to international celebrity.

2. It is acceptable to kiss at the end of the every sentence, provided it is done by text message. Any other format is just trashy.

3. If you are going to date a cartoon character girl, make sure it is Belle from Beauty and the Beast.

4. In TV, if you are not the star of the show, chances are, you're screwed!

5. If you want to see the very depths of Hell, go and sit in an Internet chat room for a period of time. Even Satan himself has to brace himself when doing so!

6. An insult becomes legendary through plagiarism.

7. History is the story as told by the winners

8. Monopoly is not realistic and thank goodness because if it was, we'd realise what a state most of our fine cities are in!

9. If you are coming to the end of your job, make sure you do something controversial and hilarious before you leave. They are giving you the boot, so make sure you leave a footprint in their company.

10. Women think about sex as much as men do. Wait, no, women think about it more.

11. Why come up with a fresh idea when you can churn out a poor sequel and make some easy money?

12. Kissing is not just a lip sport.

13. Hating someone is really easy when you think about it.

14. The human race is destroying itself with a big smile on its face

15. Record your wisest moments. Chances are they won't be of any worth until you're dead.

16. Attending an office party is mandatory if you want to keep up with the gossip but it is an inevitably horrific experience.

17. Consider carefully how you wipe your backside when you go to the toilet and don't use a front wipe method.

18. Treasure the misconceptions you have of people. It is possible that is the best opinion you could have of them.

19. Puberty is a fate worse than death.

20. Your status on a website is the prime opportunity for a comedy moment.

21. Black people are genetically the coolest people on Earth.

22. If life was a video game, all debates would be settled with death matches and to get a date, you would have to defeat a nefarious dictator's army.

23. Complaining is asking for a world of pain in the short term and a world of improvement in the long term.

24. The designated driver will insist that he has the least fun on a night out but he is the one who remembers all the funny stories and wild

adventures of the night. He is also the one who looks out for your sorry drunken carcass at the end of the night.

25. TV for children is not what it was. Those who grew up in the 80's and 90's had it oh so good!

26. Christmas is not a time of glad tidings and joy. In fact, listen to "A Fairytale in New York" by the Pogues and they will tell you exactly how Christmas feels.

27. People that walk slowly up the street, blocking your way, deserve to be punched in the back of the head.

28. Breaking up with your partner is a process that is more complex than a United Nations resolution.

29. The kind of superpower you would like to have says a lot about your character. That would be the bad side of your character usually.

30. A blonde moment is found in an intelligent woman putting a simple thing to the back of her multi-tasking mind.

31. Irish is the sexiest accent there is but I wouldn't say no to a night with a dirty Welsh accent. Just don't let a Mexican or French accent near me!

32. Walking down a High Street makes you fair game to all those kind of people that wish to leech money, time and commitment out of you. It is a test of skill and wit, dodging surveys and salesmen.

33. Having a crush on someone is costly and makes you do stupid things but it is also one of the most exciting things to have in your life.

34. People act randomly and immature in an effort to be different and only end up acting like everyone else.

35. If Sunday is the Day of the Lord, then Satan got his grubby little hands on Monday. You have got to hate Mondays!

36. Cartoons teach something false but wonderful. The good guys always win.

37. One of the worst people in your life used to be the most important person in your life. Do not try to be friends with your ex because you are better off just getting rid of them.

38. Choose your list of celebrities that you can cheat on your partner with carefully. It says a lot about you.

39. Weddings are hell!

40. Always be the one to play the practical joke rather than be the victim. You will find it is always funnier to be on that side of the joke.

41. The true answers to jokes are uncomfortable realities we would rather not face.

42. Instant messenger abbreviations are saying more than first meets the eye.

43. Don't mess with me. I know how to make you feel very small with just a few words.

44. Do not interrogate people why they are single. You will find out the reality of why you aren't and then you will realise what a fool you are.

45. Whoever decided to put the coffee Revel in the bag deserves to be executed.

46. Farting is funny.

47. The human race like to delude themselves that a mistake has a quick fix and it really doesn't.

48. Think carefully what you would do if the world was going to end tomorrow and start living every day like it might just happen. Finally then you will be living and not just surviving.

49. Finally, music can teach many things but most of those lyrics were written under the influence of narcotics, so don't heed them too closely.

Printed in the United States
210102BV00014B/299/P